Keeping Safe gives pare... a language to talk with children and teenagers about ... ...es like stranger danger, bullying, child... ...egies for keeping safe when the... ...pproach is practical, low-key ... ...e, which is a welcome relief fo... ...ard their children, but not frighten ...

  Talking through the messages in *Keeping* ... with your children will not only reduce their vulnerability, it will help them to be more confident in today's world. It's an excellent book, which all of us parents need to read.

Phil Collins
Patron of Kidscape

About the Author

Michele Elliott is a teacher, child psychologist and mother of two boys. She has worked with children and families since 1968, and is on the Advisory Councils of ChildLine and the NSPCC. She has chaired World Health Organisation and Home Office working groups about the prevention of child abuse, and has been awarded a Winston Churchill Fellowship, which she used to study the prevention of bullying. She is the author of eleven other books, including *Feeling Happy, Feeling Safe*, a colour picture book for young children, and *The Willow Street Kids* series for primary-aged children. She is often on the television and radio discussing issues of children's safety, and writes a regular column for *Family Circle* magazine. In 1984 Michele founded the registered children's charity Kidscape, which works to keep children safe from bullying, abuse and other dangers.

For free leaflets about keeping children safe, bullying or ways to cope if your child is abused, or for information about schools programmes, send a large SAE to:

Kidscape,
152 Buckingham Palace Road,
London SW1W 9TR

Keeping Safe

Michele Elliott

CORONET BOOKS
Hodder and Stoughton

To John Hadjipateras, a kind and humane man who loves children. His support has made all my work possible, and has helped keep safe thousands of children.

First published privately as *Preventing Child Sexual Assault: a parents' guide to talking with children* 1984
A new, enlarged edition first published by Bedford Square Press as *Preventing Child Sexual Assault: a practical guide to talking with children* March 1985
Reprinted April 1985
Second edition September 1985
Reprinted with corrections February 1986
Third edition published as *Keeping Safe: a practical guide to talking with children* 1986
First New English Library Paperback edition 1988
Extract on physical and emotional abuse and neglect, and the Kidscape Resource List, reproduced by kind permission of Kidscape.
New Coronet edition 1994

10 9 8 7 6 5 4 3 2 1

ISBN 0340 624825

Typeset by Phoenix Typesetting, Ilkley, West Yorkshire

Printed and bound in Great Britain by
Cox and Wyman Ltd

Hodder and Stoughton Ltd
A Division of Hodder Headline PLC
338 Euston Road
London NW1 3BH

ACKNOWLEDGEMENTS

For their help and support over many years, I would especially like to thank: Dr Arnon Bentovim, Consultant Psychiatrist at Great Ormond Street Hospital for Sick Children, Detective Chief Superintendent Peter Gwynn, headteacher Linda Frost, Dr Peter Aggleton, Co-Director of Learning About AIDS, Dan Olweus, Professor at the University of Bergen, Christina Smakowska, Librarian at the National Society for the Prevention of Cruelty to Children (NSPCC), Patricia Crumpley, lawyer and Director of the Tri-Valley Haven for Women, Sally Cooper of the Child Assault Prevention Programme, Jacqueline Sallon, friend and editor extraordinaire, and Julian Hodgeson, a gentle and intelligent man who gave me support from the beginning.

Acknowledgement is made to the Editor of *The Times Educational Supplement* for kind permission to reproduce material that appeared in my article entitled 'Caution' (*TES*, 18 April 1986).

I am indebted to the Kidscape staff, who keep me in line and work like Trojans: Jane Kilpatrick, Linda Llewellyen, Angela Glaser, Daphne Joiner, Florence Rothman and Sue Woods. And, of course, to my very supportive family, husband Edward and two sons Charles and James, who maintain a good sense of humour and put up with my continual writing and treks away from home.

A special thanks goes to Claire Rayner and Katie Boyle, both of whom have backed Kidscape from the start, and who continue to give good, sound advice.

CONTENTS

Foreword by Claire Rayner   ·   11

Introduction   13
What can we do?   14

1 **Teaching Children How to Keep Safe**   21
    What parents can do   21
    How to begin talking with children   24
    What to do next   27
    More suggestions for parents   37
    Helping teenagers to protect themselves   39
    How teachers and other adults can help   45
    More suggestions for teachers and workers   51

2 **Dealing with Child Abuse**   53
    What to look for   54
    What to do if you suspect abuse   71
    What to do if abuse occurs   75

3 **Bullying**   87

4 **Drug, Solvent and Alcohol Abuse**   105
    What parents can do   106

5 **AIDS**   113
    AIDS at school   118
    AIDS and child sexual abuse   119

6 **Amusement Arcades and Gambling**   121

7 **Videos and Computer Disks**   123

8   Other Tips for Safety   129
      When to give independence   129
      Tips on public places   130
      Telephone tips   132
      Tips on babysitters   137
      Tips for teenagers looking for part-time jobs   138

9   Conclusion   141
      Does prevention work?   141

10 Where to Get Help   145
      Abduction (parental)   145
      Abuse   146
      AIDS   147
      Alcohol   148
      Anorexia, bulimia and other eating disorders   149
      Bereavement   149
      Bullying   150
      Contraception   150
      Counselling   150
      Drugs   151
      Families   153
      Gambling   154
      Legal advice   154
      Self-defence   155
      Suicide   155
      Telephone services   155
      Victim support   156

Appendix I: 'What if' Questions   157
      'What if?' questions to ask your children   158
      'What if?' questions to ask your teens   160

Appendix II: Questionnaire for Young Teenagers   165
      Questions   165
      Answers   167

Appendix III: Questions for Older Teenagers   171
      Questions   171
      Answers   174

Appendix IV: Sources of Information 181
  Sources of information 181
  Books for children 181
  Books for teens 182
  Books for adults 183
  Training package for front-line carers 186
  Kidscape child-protection schools programmes 187
  Talking books for the blind 187

FOREWORD by Claire Rayner

Back in the early 1950s, first as a young nurse and then, later, as a departmental sister in a busy North London Paediatric Unit, I discovered a fact that was deeply distressing. A great many children and young people were suffering abuse of various kinds at the hands of the adults in their lives who were supposed to be caring for them. My first instinct was to look after the children I met who had so suffered – after all, that was why I was a nurse; to offer care – the second, to be angry with the adults who perpetrated the abuse and to want to punish them, and the third was to tell everyone all about it so that children could be alerted and therefore be able to protect themselves.

I soon learned that of those three responses only one could really be applied: I could look after the children if they came into our wards. But I couldn't express my anger at the adults, for there was little proof of what the children told us had happened to them (and too many in authority then chose to regard them as liars) and I certainly couldn't publicise the matter. The general feeling around the hospital, and, I know, the world at large, was that this was something you absolutely didn't talk about.

Once I became a medical journalist and started to deal with letters from the general public asking for help for their manifold problems, I discovered that the problem of child-hood abuse was even more widespread than I had realised *and always had been*. I had letters from people in their sixties and seventies and older still who were suffering psychological damage because of what had been done to them in childhood. Once again I tried to publicise the matter, but this time I met editorial resistance rather than the medical resistance of my nursing days. This was something we didn't talk about . . .

Well, I persisted, as did other journalists and enlightened doctors, and gradually we have between us broken down the wall of silence. We can and do admit that child abuse goes on and that children need help to avoid or resist it. And we now also realise that we must give such help if only so that the *chain* of abuse can be broken. Because, tragically, so often in the history of abusing adults is found the experience of childhood abuse. As the child received, so the adult gives . . .

Now I can see that one of my other wishes from the fifties is being granted – to give all the children the care they need. The best sort of care, which is not the sort that is applied from outside in the form of adult controls, adult watchfulness and adult anxiety (though these have their place) but in the form of solid information for the children themselves. The child who understands the risks the world carries and who is given strategies to deal with them is the best-armoured child there can be. Innocence is never enhanced by ignorance, as people used to think. It is possible to arm children with all sorts of knowledge without damaging their intrinsic good-heartedness and responsiveness to other good and caring people. That is the great gift that Michele Elliott offers children in this, her excellent book. With its help, our children will not only be safer; they will grow up to be genuinely caring and protective adults. And one day we must all hope there will be less need for my second wish – to punish the adults who perpetrate the abuse. Because not only will they be fewer, but, we *hope*, accessible to cure. Reading this book is necessary for all of us. We all have a lot to learn, and these pages can provide it.

Claire Rayner

INTRODUCTION

Things seemed so different when I was a child. I remember leaving early in the morning with a packed lunch of jam sandwiches and not a care. Mum would wave, and tell us to be careful and not to get into trouble. The only thing we had to do was be 'back before dark'. Of course, we were warned about strangers, but you also politely said hello if any adult talked to you.

Perhaps I look back with rose-tinted glasses to a childhood that seems now to have been safer and kinder than that faced by my own children. We know now that bullying and child abuse were happening to children then just as they are now. But the fear of abduction or the threat of drugs, AIDS and video nasties didn't worry us or our parents. And the horrifying news of a child being murdered was rarer then than it is today.

Maybe we are paranoid, but nowadays not only is it frightening to let our children go to the park on their own for an hour or two, but we wonder if it is safe to ask them to run a quick errand to the corner shop.

I vividly remember when I relented to my eldest son's request to go, on his own, to the paper shop. We lived on the sixth floor of a block of flats. I waved goodbye as he got into the lift, rushed down the stairs and hid behind the front door, watching him carefully cross the road. I continued to peer out from behind the door until he got safely back across the road, then ran puffing up the stairs in time to gasp a greeting as he came out of the lift.

We all feel that children are vulnerable. Letting them out

of sight often terrifies us (see When to Give Independence, p. 129–30). Some children do go missing; a small number of children are abducted and murdered. It is no use telling parents that the chances are one in a million, that psychopaths are few and far between, and that children are far more likely to be harmed by someone they know (dealt with in the next section of this book). All these statements are true, but that won't stop us from worrying.

Seeing those innocent young faces on the news, hearing their parents' anguish, and knowing that 'there but for the grace of God goes my child', brings a chill of dread to all of us. We can help both ourselves and our children if we can teach them the best ways to deal with potentially dangerous situations.

What can we do?

WRAP THEM UP IN COTTON WOOL

One way to keep children safe is never to let them out of your sight. Sometimes, for a short time, there are valid reasons for this. One father told me that his daughter was playing in the garden when a man drove up and attempted to snatch her. Later that day, this same man tried again to take another child from a local playground. The father said he watched his child constantly and was really worried because the man in the car had not been caught. Obviously, this father was wise under the circumstances.

However, pity the child who is never given any freedom to learn to deal with the world. We have to let our children out. We won't always be there, and they need to develop self-confidence.

TEACH THEM HOW TO COPE

What do you do when your children want more freedom than you think they can handle? When they say things like, 'You treat me like a baby!' or 'Everyone else gets to stay out until midnight' or 'All my friends go to the shops alone.'

It is natural for children to try to gain that extra bit of independence, but we don't have to give in when we know that they should not be roaming the streets or be out after dark. We should resist those unreasonable demands, exhausting though it may be.

We must, however, let children spread their wings. We owe it to them to teach them how to cope in the world and how to develop strategies to use in case someone tries to harm them.

But talking about what to do isn't enough. We don't just tell children to look both ways before crossing the road, we show them by taking them by the hand and practising. The same applies when teaching children about yelling, running and even kicking to get out of a dangerous situation: don't just say it, get them to do it until you are satisfied that they could summon up a really convincing yell at anyone who tries to molest them.

Yelling

Most children are experts in yelling – ask any parent. The difference here is that you need to teach them to yell in a particular way that will attract attention and not sound feeble. The 'I'm in danger' yell should sound like a foghorn. It comes not from the throat, but from deep in the stomach. The advantage of this yell is that it does not get 'frozen' in your throat if you are frightened. It jumps out and can startle an attacker away because it is so unexpected. Try putting your hand on your stomach so you can feel the source of the yell, take a deep breath, and let the yell flow out, loud and clear. Practise several times and then do it with your children. Don't feel embarrassed; it could save your child's life and bring help.

Running

We always tell children to run away from danger, but most people are frozen still when something happens. It helps if you have actually practised 'running away' with your children. Pretend that you are trying to grab them (make it a game if the children are young, as you probably do already), and tell them to run away as fast as they can. Practise yelling and running at the same time. A child who has practised will stand a better chance of reacting than one who has only been told what to do. Teenagers should definitely practise, too, but you may have difficulty convincing them. Try making them yell and run for their pocket money!

If a child is in a wheelchair or gets around with crutches or other aids, practise getting away and yelling, if possible, and trying to attract attention. If they have communication difficulties, help children practise ways to sign or signal distress. Unfortunately, all children are vulnerable and need strategies.

Keeping your distance

We always tell children not to go with strangers and not to talk with them when they are on their own. One way to help ensure that they remember this rule is to tell them to keep their distance should a stranger come towards them and try to strike up a conversation, or motion them to come over to a car. Keeping several arms' lengths away can prevent children from being grabbed. Demonstrate to your child and practise.

Pretending not to hear

Anyone with a spouse or partner or teenager will marvel at his or her ability to tune you out when you have an urgent request like setting the table or taking out the rubbish. Use this as an example when explaining to children that a good defence if they are approached by a stranger when they are alone is simply to pretend not to hear and to keep going. If the person persists and follows them, then she or he is probably up to no good and it is best to yell and run.

Kicking

In the first few seconds of an attack, a child who has been taught to react quickly may have an advantage. The attacker may presume that the child will be passive and scared, so an immediate, noisy and active response could give a child enough time to get away, which is the object. Having practised yelling and getting away, try *carefully* practising a swift kick to the shins or knee of the attacker. I say carefully because you could end up bruised for life by your enthusiastic child!

If a child is grabbed from behind, she or he can kick the attacker's knee in a quick backward motion, scrape down the inside of the attacker's leg, stomp quite hard on the attacker's foot (instep) and then run away. Another technique for older children is to bring the elbow into the attacker's stomach or groin and run. The goal is to startle or hurt the attacker and then to run away.

Getting away from an attacker

Explain to children that getting away is the whole reason for practising these strategies and that they should *never* chase after an attacker. When talking to young children about what they could do if someone tried to grab them, they often say they would get the attacker and tie him up – sometimes with the help of a super-hero. Of course, this is a natural childish fantasy and children would most likely not go after someone much bigger than themselves. But we do need to emphasise to all children and teenagers that

they need to get away to safety, and leave the capture
of the attacker to the police.

Getting away from a flasher

Twelve-year-old David was in the park when a man
exposed himself to the boy. David was too terrified
to move. Finally the man ran off, leaving David
rooted to the spot. When he gained his composure,
David hurried home, but was too embarrassed to
tell anyone what had happened.

Children need to know that there are some weirdos in the
world who do things that give them a thrill but make no
sense to the rest of us (see also Obscene Calls, p. 134–5).
The above suggestions for yelling and getting away are useful
if there are people around. Another suggestion might be
simply to turn quickly and get away without saying anything. Most flashers are just that – flashers – they don't
usually try to touch the person they are confronting. In
these circumstances, therefore, a silent, quick escape is an
effective course of action. Whatever strategy the child uses,
however, the object is to get away quickly.

The importance of practice

One mother rang to tell me that her nine-year-old son
had been on his way home from school when a man
and a woman in a car had asked for directions. Her
son, Sam, made the mistake of going over to the car,
even though she had practised keeping his distance
with him. The woman leant out of the window to
show Sam a map and the man came around the car,
behind Sam, and tried to shove him into the back
seat. Sam kicked at him, twisted away, yelled, and
then ran as fast as he could all the way to school,
where he collapsed in a heap of jelly.

Sam later said that although he shouldn't have gone up to the car, all the practising he had done with his mother had automatically come back to him. He hadn't thought about it – he'd just done it. The mother was grateful and said that practising had literally saved her son's life, although she needed to do more work with him on 'keeping your distance'.

Telephoning

If Sam had not managed to get away at first but had escaped later, knowing how he could contact his parents might have been important. Most children know how to ring on their own home telephone, but many have never been taught how to use a public telephone and do not know that you can make an emergency call or that you can telephone the operator and be connected to home without having any money. Practise using public telephones: pretend to dial 999 or pretend that you are the operator and have your child ask to place a reverse-charge call to your number. There is no need to connect this with abduction because it makes sense for children to know how to use public telephones.

If you have custody of your children and are concerned that their other parent might try to abduct them, be sure your children know about using the telephone to contact you. If their other parent is from another country, try to teach your children how to telephone you from overseas, if this is possible (see Where to Get Help, p. 145).

BE POSITIVE

The positive way to look at this problem of child safety and the continuous reporting of attacks on children is that, thankfully, it is still rare for a child to be abducted and murdered by a stranger. But it does happen, and the important thing to remember is that we can help our children to help themselves. Teach your children these practical and potentially life-saving strategies, and when they ask 'Can I go out?', you can answer: 'Yes, but remember to run away quickly if anyone tries to grab you. Don't talk to strangers, and yell your head off if you feel in danger. Have a good time and be home before dark.'

1

TEACHING CHILDREN HOW TO KEEP SAFE

What parents can do

Although stranger danger is a big concern for parents, there are other dangers that are more likely to cause problems for children. Bullying, child abuse, drugs, abduction and other worries all leave us parents with a dilemma. We need to warn children about such dangers, but we don't want to destroy their trust and innocence. There is a way to solve the problem and that is to give children as much information as they need to be safe, without overwhelming them with fear or unnecessary details. If we turn to keeping children as safe as possible from child abuse, for example, there are some things most parents already do, or try to do, that will help.

Fortunately, most children do not become victims of abuse, just as most children do not become victims of drownings or traffic accidents. However, in the same way that parents teach children how to swim or cross the road, we can teach children practical ways to keep safe from abuse and to tell us if something is happening. This can be done in a manner that is neither frightening nor unrealistic.

Children need to know how to get help, to recognise that touching should not be kept secret, to realise that it is all right to say no when anyone tries to do something which makes them frightened or confused, that there are ways to avoid dangerous situations and that we want to know if anything happens. It is the *lack* of information that makes children vulnerable.

Unfortunately, child abuse knows no boundaries; it can happen to children within every neighbourhood, every class and every racial background. It can happen to children with disabilities or children in care or in foster homes. The list is endless. What we can do is talk to children about prevention and teach children according to their level of understanding, age and circumstances at the very least how to seek help and at best how to prevent abuse.

We are not expecting children to take full responsibility for keeping themselves safe. It is our responsibility, but it is their right to be safe, and preventive techniques not only reduce their vulnerability, but also make them more confident.

ENCOURAGE CHILDREN TO EXPRESS THEIR FEELINGS

Parents want to help their children grow into happy and confident adults. A child's ability or inclination to trust, to feel good about achievements, to share, and to be confident are learned from parents and other people with whom the child comes into contact.

These experiences form the basis for children learning strategies for keeping safe. This learning process starts from the time they are very young. For example, the best way for a child to learn to differentiate between furtive, false affection and normal, everyday affection is to experience open, loving hugs and kisses and positive relationships with adults.

But even this normal, healthy affection is becoming a problem for some people in the light of concern about sexual abuse. Fathers and other men are starting to feel uneasy about hugging or touching children, lest their affection be wrongly interpreted. One father said he was now worried when his children piled into bed for an early-morning cuddle. Another felt himself holding back when his son wanted a goodnight kiss.

This kind of attitude makes men uncomfortable and harms children. Children need affection – from men and women.

Frederick II, a thirteenth-century king, once conducted an experiment in which he told foster mothers and nurses to feed and bathe the babies in their care, but not to speak to them or cuddle them. According to the medieval writer Salimbene, Frederick wanted to find out what kind of speech and manner the children would have without ever being taught. The experiment ended tragically, as all the babies died!

Not all children who are deprived of love die, but children do need a strong foundation of love for building their confidence and ability to cope. They thrive on our cuddles and we certainly need theirs. So when children seek affection and it is given freely and openly, no one should feel uneasy.

By extending this openness to communication between parents and children, we can encourage children to tell us if anything frightening or untoward happens to them, thereby allowing us to help. But to do this we must allow and, indeed, encourage children to express their feelings.

Children are often made to believe that they are not allowed to have feelings or that their feelings are unimportant. For example, if Brian comes home with a skinned, bleeding knee and the response is, 'For goodness' sake, Brian, stop crying. It doesn't hurt!', who is Brian to believe – his own feelings or this message? Will Brian then tell when something else happens or will he expect to be told, 'Don't be so silly!'? The same applies if children dislike someone and are told 'it is not polite to say no'. What will they do if someone asks them to get into a car, to play a secret game or to try drugs?

What about being forced to kiss people goodbye or endure unwanted tickling? We cannot teach children to trust their feelings and tell us if they feel unsafe while at the same time making them suppress those very feelings.

Encouraging children to trust and to express their feelings, and believing them when they do, is the basis for learning any strategies for keeping safe, whether the problem is bullies, possible sexual abuse or drugs.

How to begin talking with children

There are several ways to begin a conversation with children about keeping safe. Two simple and direct methods that have worked most successfully involve discussing personal safety rights, or talking about touching that feels good, safe and comfortable, and touching that feels bad, unsafe, or is secretive.

DISCUSS THE RIGHT TO BE SAFE

Explain to children that everyone has rights that should not be taken away from them. Start with simple ideas such as the right to breathe, eat, sleep, play or go to the toilet. Ask children what would happen if the right to eat was taken away from them. Would that create problems? What if they were not allowed to go to the toilet?

Children should be encouraged to think about what would happen in order to start them using their own judgement. Ask them to think of ways to get their rights back. One child said that if she were not allowed to eat, she would collect berries. Another said that he would go on strike and picket his house with a sign saying 'Unfair to children'.

After children clearly understand this concept, use it to discuss the right to be safe. Ask them when they feel safe, and ask them to give specific examples such as 'when my parents tuck me into bed with a goodnight kiss' or 'when playing with my friends' or 'when reading a story with Mummy'. One five-year-old said that being safe was 'not having to stay with the lions in the zoo'. Explain that sometimes people try to take away the rights of others, including the right to be safe.

Emphasise to children that they should say no and get help when someone tries to take away their rights and that you will support them in this. Make sure that children understand that the right to be safe includes the right to say what happens to their own bodies. (See the later suggestions about saying no and talking with children about their bodies.)

DISCUSS SAFE TOUCHES AND UNSAFE TOUCHES

Another approach is to begin with an explanation of touching that feels safe and touching that feels unsafe, which the child may refer to as good or bad touches. You can introduce this by talking about how nice a hug or kiss can be and by asking children how they would show someone they love them (without giving a tangible gift such as a puppy or toy). One child said he would give someone he loved a thousand hugs and kisses every day. If you have a pet, ask children what kind of touches the pet likes and dislikes. Then ask what kind of touches children like and dislike. Children may say they like soft hugs and big kisses. They often mention that tickling is fun, but not too much or for too long. Many children relate that they hate being patted on the head.

Explain that children have the right to say no, even to someone they love, if they do not like a touch or a kiss. This means that children should not be forced to be affectionate with anyone, even their own parents.

Parents can help their children politely to refuse kisses or hugs that make them uncomfortable, even in an everyday situation. If necessary, explain that your child is going through a 'shy stage' or be totally honest and say that your child is learning to say no to requests that make him or her uncomfortable. If we force children to be affectionate because we as adults are embarrassed if they are not, we are not helping them. Children must begin to trust their own feelings and judgement if they are to learn to keep themselves safe.

This also means that children will have to learn that there are times when the rules of being polite do not apply and it might be necessary to break them.

There are many different cultural customs about hugging, kissing and touching. There is no reason for these to change. However, in any culture it is inappropriate for an adult to seek contact with children as a result of his or her own sexual needs or if the adult is seeking to be sexually stimulated by the contact.

TEACH CHILDREN TO SAY NO

Instead of teaching children to listen to and obey all adults without question, tell them that they have your permission and support to say no to protect themselves. Help them to practise saying no in an assertive way, because it is very difficult for most children to say no to an adult.

In the classroom or at home, adults can help children to learn to say no by asking if it is easy to say no to someone older. Children usually say that it is difficult to refuse an adult's request or command. Explain that you are going to help them practise saying no. This will enable them to say no if someone asks them to do anything that makes them confused or uncomfortable. Start with questions children can easily say no to, such as:

Adult: 'Do you like cheese?'
Child: 'No.'
Adult: 'Wouldn't you like a cheese sandwich?'
Child: 'No.' (Said from a distance.)

Proceed to questions requiring caution:

Adult: 'Can you tell me how to get to the cinema?'
Child: 'No.'

Most adults do not ask children for directions, so it is safer to tell children not to get involved. Tell children that they should not enter into conversation, nor give reasons for not talking. If an adult comes close, the child should move quickly away and say nothing.

Children can offer suggestions, and the idea of saying no in an assertive way can be learned in a safe environment. Practising will help to make saying no automatic in a potentially dangerous situation. Along with refusing to keep secrets and knowing about bad touching, saying no can be an especially effective deterrent against the non-violent offender who is known to the child. One man who had molested three of his four children was asked why he did not abuse the fourth. 'She said "no",' was his answer.

However, it is not always possible for a child to say no because of fear or the threat of violence. It may be necessary for the child to comply with the adult's demand and then seek help by telling. When teaching children to say no, they should be told that there may be times when they cannot and that you will understand and support them. The most important message is that you want them to be safe.

What to do next

TALK TO CHILDREN ABOUT THEIR BODIES

Explain to children that their bodies are their own and that no one should touch them in a way that makes them confused or uncomfortable. Help them understand that this means their whole body, from the top of their head to their toes, as well as the private parts of their bodies. Teach children the correct names of their private parts. However, if this makes you uncomfortable, another explanation is 'those parts covered by your bathing suit'. (Even if you do teach your children the correct names, they usually learn a variety of terms at school. My children went to school with penises and came home with willies!)

The terms you use are not nearly as important as teaching children that they have the right to control what happens to their bodies. There is no need to give children too much information, which could frighten them. But even young children have a strong sense of their own identity and what they like and dislike.

TALK ABOUT SAFE SECRETS VERSUS UNSAFE SECRETS

Since people who abuse children often depend upon children's willingness to keep secrets, it is extremely effective to teach children, even very young ones, to say no to this request.

In some families, children are taught to keep surprises, but never to keep secrets. Another method is to teach children the difference between safe and unsafe secrets. Ask children to suggest a safe secret. They will probably mention a birthday present, or surprise party, or Mummy having another baby. See if they can describe an unsafe secret. Some examples that children have offered are: 'Daddy and Mummy are fighting', 'knowing your friend has taken something from a shop', or 'a bully who takes away your money and you are too scared to tell'.

When children understand the difference between safe and unsafe secrets, they are ready to be taught that no one should ask them to keep touching a secret. This applies to all touching, even if it feels good. Tell children that they should always tell a trusted adult if anyone asks them to keep such a secret. Help children make a list of people they feel they can talk to if they have a problem, or let them make a list by themselves.

One difficulty in dealing with child sexual abuse is that sometimes the victims experience physical pleasure. This often compounds the confusion and makes the children feel that they are accomplices and that their bodies have betrayed them. An added problem may be that the abuser is also the only person from whom the child is receiving any type of affection, however inappropriate. This is particularly true if the abuser is a member of the child's family. By telling children that no touches, hugs or kisses should be kept secret, you are helping them to define the boundaries and giving them permission to seek adult help. Children may feel responsible or even guilty about what has happened and you must try to give them a way of telling in order to help to relieve that burden.

ENCOURAGE CHILDREN TO TELL

Assure your children that no matter what happens you will not be angry with them and that you want them to tell you of any incident. Explain the difference between telling tales to get someone into trouble and getting help when someone is threatening their safety. Ask children to give examples of telling tales, such as running to the teacher because another child is using the swings when they want to swing. Then talk about dangerous situations in which a child should get help. One child described a time when his bicycle had been taken from him and the teenager threatened him with a beating if he told anyone.

Explain to children that even if they break a home or school rule that leads to them getting into difficulty, you still want to know and you will not blame them. An eleven-year-old girl broke the family rule about going through the park to get home after school. A man forced her into the bushes and indecently assaulted her. He told her he would find her and kill her if she told someone. She eventually told her parents, who immediately comforted her and assured her that it was the offender who was guilty, not her. They did not say, 'See what happens when you don't listen?' The child knew she should not have gone across the park, but to have made her feel guilty would not have been helpful.

By giving your children the assurance that you will support them, no matter what circumstances preceded the incident, you will help them to cope better with an assault, should it occur. If you do not give this kind of assurance and mean it, your children will not tell you for fear that you will be angry with them.

Since children often feel that adults do not believe them, encourage children to keep telling until someone does and the children get help.

CAUTION ABOUT TELLING

One freely available leaflet advises parents to tell their children to say to someone who is hurting them: 'I'm going to tell!' This is not wise because it could lead to real physical harm. It is one thing to say no when possible, quite another to threaten an offender with disclosure. Be certain that you explain to children and to young people not to say to the offender that they will tell, but to get away first, no matter what they have to promise. They can then wait until they feel safe to talk.

TALK ABOUT PRESENTS VERSUS BRIBES

Child molesters, whether adults known to children or strangers, often offer children bribes in exchange for sexual favours. Children should be taught what bribes are and what those who offer bribes seek to accomplish.

Ask children to give you examples of gifts, such as birthday or holiday presents given to celebrate a happy occasion. These gifts may be kept as a surprise before they are given, but are not kept a secret when they are received. Explain that gifts and bribes are different. The message that children need to learn is that gifts are given freely with no conditions and that bribes are given to make them do something they do not want to do.

One child said that his teacher 'bribed' him with gold stars to do his maths, which he didn't want to do. The child definitely understood the concept of bribery, but it is the secretive, furtive element of 'don't tell anyone and I'll give you some sweets' that should be emphasised.

TALK ABOUT TRICKS

Explain to children that some people, both known adults and strangers, might try to trick them by offering them a present, money, sweets or a trip to the zoo or cinema to make them do something they don't like. Tell them that if that happens they should say something like, 'I must ask Mum/Dad/my teacher', and then get away quickly to seek help.

A common trick used by molesters is, 'Your mum is sick and asked me to take you to her'. One suggestion that many parents have used is to have a codeword known only to the parents and children. If you must send someone to collect children in an emergency, the person sent would use the agreed code.

Tell children that you want to be told if anyone offers them a bribe or tries to trick them.

DO NOT DEFINE PEOPLE AS GOOD OR BAD

If children think only bad people hurt them, they will not be prepared for the person who approaches them in a manner that gains their trust. By teaching them the danger signs, you will be protecting them far better than if you tell them to watch out for 'bad' people. One method of relating this is to explain that people have good and bad in them and sometimes even good people do things we do not like.

> The mother of a ten-year-old boy said that her son had been taught to say no to strangers and was confident that he could take care of himself. One afternoon after school when the boy was alone, a man wearing a business suit and carrying a briefcase knocked on the door. The boy opened the door, using the safety chain. The man claimed that he was taking his pregnant wife to the hospital, their car had broken down and he had to telephone for an ambulance. The boy offered to telephone for him, but the man insisted that this was an emergency and there was no time to spare. The boy let him in and was sexually assaulted. His mother said that her son told her afterwards that the man had not seemed to be a 'bad person' because he was dressed 'like Daddy and did not look like a stranger'.

Most children do not understand the concept of 'stranger'. When asked to describe strangers, children will say they are dirty, weird, ugly, smelly and suspicious. Anyone who fits a child's concept of 'nice' is not a stranger. Even if they understand that strangers are people you do not know, children quickly take people out of this category.

It is important to emphasise that they should get away if anyone tries to do something that makes them frightened or confused. Tell children that if anyone approaches them and tries to talk to them when they are on their own, they should pretend not to hear and walk away, saying nothing. It is better to do that and perhaps hurt someone's feelings than to take a chance and get hurt oneself.

ANSWER CHILDREN'S QUESTIONS

When children are concerned about television programmes, nightmares, newspaper reports or tragedies, answer their questions carefully and sensitively without dismissing their feelings or denying the reality of the situation. This helps children to trust their own feelings and judgement and is better than telling them not to worry. Children will not share their feelings if they are not taken seriously.

However, there is no need to frighten children with too much information. Understand what children are really asking and give them the facts gradually until they are satisfied with the answer. For example, one five-year-old girl asked her mother what rape was because she heard the word on television. The mother's response was to find out what her daughter thought it was and to proceed from there. In this case the explanation that it meant someone touching her private parts in a way she did not like was all that was needed. If an older child asked the same question, he or she would probably need more information and a fuller explanation. Explaining instead of avoiding is the important message so that children will feel confident about asking questions because they will know that they will receive honest answers.

BELIEVE YOUR CHILDREN

Children rarely lie about sexual abuse that has occurred: they do not have the language or experience to invent. Later, however, they may deny that abuse took place in order to protect someone they love or because they are afraid. Children may also get the details confused because of the traumatic nature of what has happened. When dealing with children, question gently but do not interrogate.

Ask for the reasons when children do not want to go to someone's house or do not like a babysitter, or when their behaviour patterns change dramatically (see p. 54–60). Gently draw out more information about comments such as 'I don't like the way John teases me' or 'The man at the shop acts funny'. Although these comments usually indicate something harmless, parents must learn to be sensitive to what their children are trying to say. One child told her mother that her uncle teased her and she didn't like it. The mother responded that everyone gets teased growing up and she would have to get used to it. The child was very upset, but did not say anything else. Several months later, the girl was diagnosed as having gonorrhoea of the throat. Her uncle had called it teasing and she was too young to know better.

Create an atmosphere of trust in which children know they will be listened to and believed. They will then be encouraged to share their concerns and potentially harmful situations can thereby be avoided.

PLAY 'WHAT IF?' GAMES

Children often ask 'What would happen if . . . ?' type questions, which parents can turn into a fun learning game. Instead of answering immediately, ask your children what they think would happen. This gives them a chance to test their ideas and judgement about the world. Parents can initiate questions as well, but should be careful not to ask questions that may frighten children.

With young children it might be better to start with something like 'What would you do if a monkey came to the door?' Then, if the child is interested, ask other questions that are appropriate to his or her age. (Since the monkey is a stranger, by the way, the child should not let it in!) This can lead to a discussion of who would be let in: what if someone was dressed like Daddy or said Mummy was ill, for example? Questions like 'What if someone you know tries to touch you in a way you do not like?' should be included when the child is ready.

Playing 'What if?' games, either at home or in school, is a good way for children to learn many concepts. You can start with a variety of situations not related to assaults. For example:

Adult: 'What if you saw smoke coming from your neighbour's house?'
Child: 'I would ring the fire brigade.'
Adult: 'How would you do that? Show me.'

This would be a good way to teach a child about making 999 calls (see p. 132–133). Examples of preventive 'What if?' games might be:

Adult: 'What if someone said he or she was a friend of Daddy's and asked you to go with him or her to a house?'
Child: 'I would not go and would run away if anyone got too close. I would tell a grown-up what had happened.'

When the children are prepared for the more sensitive questions, ask:

Adult: 'What if a babysitter or relative you liked asked you to play secret games, and offered to let you stay up late, or to give you a present or money?'
Child: 'I would say that I am not allowed to keep secrets.'
Adult: 'What if the person insisted?'
Child: 'I would say no. When it was safe, I would tell.'
Adult: 'Well done!'

One mother told me how she got off a bus with her baby and was turning around to collect her other child when the bus left. Eventually she was reunited with the child, but after much anxiety and tears all round.

So, another 'What if?' question might be:

Adult: 'What would you do if we were on a bus or tube and somehow I got off and you did not?'
Child: 'I would get off and meet you at the very next bus stop, or I would get off at the next underground station and stay on the platform and tell the station manager what had happened.'
Adult: 'What would you do if you accidentally got off at a stop before me?'

Child: 'I would stay there and wait for you to come and collect me.'

Alternatively, you may want to give different instructions, such as stay on the bus and tell the conductor what has happened. What you decide will depend upon the age of your children and the locality in which you usually travel.

Adult: 'What would you do if you were lost?'
Child: 'I would stay at the place I was and wait for you to find me. I would tell the person in charge of the store what had happened, but not leave or go outside.' (The store is probably a safe place to wait.)

The common message here is for the child to wait for the adult to collect him or her, rather than for the child to set out in search of the adult.

When travelling, shopping or taking children to a busy place, it is important to have a plan about what to do and where to meet should you become separated. This will give everyone a strategy and hopefully result in a quick reunion.

An example when shopping might be:

Adult: 'If we get lost from each other, we will meet at the water fountain.'

Be sure actually to show the meeting place to the children so that they are not confused. Emphasise that they should not go outside the shop or area. These kind of instructions are becoming more necessary as we take children to theme parks and other places where we and they are not familiar with the locality.

Always try to praise ideas children have about keeping themselves safe. This encourages them to continue to think creatively. Other suggested topics for 'What if?' games might be what to do if:

- you lost your way

- you saw a road accident

- a stranger tried to talk to you when you were on your own

- you went to the shop to buy bread, but the shop had run out

- you were home alone and someone came to the door. (Children should never be left home alone, but they need to know what to do should this occur.)

Have children make up 'What if?' questions for each other and for you. (See p. 157–163 for additional ideas of 'What if?' questions.)

GIVE CHILDREN PERMISSION TO BREAK RULES

If children find themselves in a difficult situation, they may not be able to deal with it because they feel restrained by all the everyday rules they have been taught. In teaching children to keep themselves safe, we must tell them that there are exceptions to every rule.

For example, children are taught to be polite, not to lie, not to tell tales, and certainly not to resist adults. Yet to keep themselves safe children may need to break one or more of these rules. Parents should discuss this with their children (by using the 'What if?' game) and give them permission to make exceptions.

The most important message you can teach children is that they have the right to use any method to keep themselves safe in a potentially dangerous situation. Again, using language appropriate to their age, tell children it is all right not to answer the door, to say no to someone they love, to yell, run, bite, kick, lie, break a window, etc. Remind them that the object is always to run, get away and seek adult help. Give them your permission to break all rules to protect themselves and tell them you will support them.

The father of six-year-old Adam who was abducted and murdered said:

> 'Adam was a model child, he never even went to the park by himself. He never disobeyed, never. I taught him to listen to adults, to respect his elders and to be a little gentleman. I never taught him how to scream. He might be alive if he had screamed.'

More suggestions for parents

- Teach children their full names, addresses and telephone numbers. If children are lost, they will know how to contact you. This is also helpful should they need to make an emergency telephone call.

- Do not teach children to answer the telephone by repeating their name or telephone number. If an obscene or 'heavy breather' caller knows the child's name, he can use it to gain his or her confidence or to frighten the child. If the caller has dialled at random and the child gives your number, the caller can then ring again.

- Help children practise making an emergency telephone call (see p. 133).

- Evaluate children's regular walking routes and playing places. This will help children to know the best ways to get home and where it is safest to play. Children should avoid isolated play places and paths, and being out at night alone.

- Do not put names on the outside of children's clothes or books. This gives an adult who is intending to harm a child an advantage. Children might be confused if someone they do not know suddenly says hello using their name. It makes them think that the stranger knows them.

- Watch for negative reactions to people and explore suspicious comments children may make about adults, older children or teenagers, babysitters, etc. Most of the time there will be a harmless reason, such as the child-minder made the child take a nap when the child did not want to. However, there could be other reasons. One child said she hated the neighbour's hamster and did not want to go there any more. The parents eventually learned that the neighbour had been interfering with her and she did not know how to talk about what was happening.

• Help children establish a network of trusted adults to whom they can turn for help.

• Teach children never to answer the door when at home alone or admit over the telephone to being alone. Practise telephone answers such as 'My mother is in the bath. If you will leave your number, she will ring you back.'

• Play games involving observation skills such as looking at objects on a tray for ten seconds and recalling them from memory. Ask a member of the family to come into the room for ten seconds, then leave. Try to recall as many details as possible about him or her. While travelling in the car, see who can call out registration numbers on red cars etc. These observation skills are useful in everyday life, but may also be vital in describing what happened or what someone looked like if a child is attacked.

• Tell children not to react to flashers. Many children report being flashed at on the underground, near playgroups, in parks and at bus stops. It can be quite terrifying and lead to nightmares and other problems. Explain that the person doing this is looking for a reaction, even if it is laughter or rude comments. The very best thing to do is not to look, then to get away from the situation as soon as possible and immediately tell an adult.

One eleven-year-old girl was standing at her bus stop when a man came up to her and flashed. She had the presence of mind to walk away quickly into a shop, but she got a good description of the man and the police were able to act on her information. She later reported that she

had not been frightened and did not panic because she knew what to do.
...Again, giving children strategies is far better than making them fearful.

- Check with other parents concerning your babysitter's reliability and behaviour (see p. 137–138).

- If your child has a nightmare and is afraid to go back to sleep, turn on the light and search the room with him or her. This will comfort the child far more than saying there is nothing there. It will also assure your child that you listen and believe what he or she says and that you are prepared to intervene actively to help. This kind of listening could be quite important for future communication.

    However, make sure that this is comforting to your child and that he or she doesn't end up thinking you believe that it is possible for monsters to be in the wardrobe.

- Hug and kiss your children. Most child molesters never had good hugs and kisses: in one American study 80 per cent were found to have been molested themselves as children, either physically or sexually. For children, those appropriate touches, hugs and kisses are the best gifts we can give them.

In spite of taking precautions, it is not always possible to prevent a child from being harmed. Remember that if someone harms a child, it is always the offender's fault, and never the fault of the child or the person trying to keep the child safe.

Helping teenagers to protect themselves

While parents want their teenagers to be independent, it is obvious that this group also needs preventive tactics to deal with common assault problems. The most frequent problem at this age is acquaintance or date rape. Too often teenagers are afraid to hurt someone's feelings, or do not want to look foolish in front of their friends, or just do not expect someone they know to betray their trust. Therefore they may end up in a dangerous situation not knowing what to do.

> Susan, eighteen years old, was at a staff Christmas party with people from the firm where she had worked for over a year. After she had drunk too much, her twenty-seven-year-old manager insisted on driving her home. He easily persuaded her to stop and have a cup of coffee at his flat so that her parents would not see her in such a state. Once in the flat, he threatened her, raped her seven times and left her unconscious. She woke up after he had passed out, left the flat, took a taxi home and never went back to her job. She also never told anyone or reported it to the police because, 'I went with him to the flat. The police would not believe me if I said it was rape.' Although she knows her parents would believe her, she is afraid that her father would kill the man and that her parents would worry about her every time she went out. Susan is still angry, hurt, confused and frightened by the incident.

WHAT YOU SHOULD DISCUSS

Setting limits

By deciding what needs and limits they have, teenagers will be in a better position to determine if they are getting into a situation beyond their control. These limits will change depending on the person they are with and on the teenager's age and maturity. By thinking about their own boundaries, teenagers will begin to test and trust their judgement, an important tool in keeping safe.

Setting limits can include deciding what to do if asked by friends or acquaintances to go along with something teenagers either like or do not really like or feel comfortable about. What if a group of friends want to go to the cinema, have a party, go to a pub, get drunk, shoplift, try drugs, go to a disco, go somewhere for a 'kiss and cuddle', or find some girls or boys 'ready for action'? Teenagers should think about what they want before the opportunities are presented to them.

Communicating these limits

Teenagers need to be told to communicate their limits to others: boyfriends, girlfriends, friends or acquaintances. Although peer-group pressure is strong at this age, planning in advance makes saying no easier. For younger teenagers, using parents as an excuse sometimes helps: 'My mum won't let me . . .' Parents should not be misled by their teenagers' rebellious poses; many teenagers are secretly grateful to place the 'blame' on their parents.

Trusting intuition

Often teenagers do not trust their own feelings and judgement. Though they may sense they are getting into a difficult situation, they have not thought out what to do or do not want to appear silly in front of friends, so they go along until it is too late. By learning to trust that inner feeling, teenagers can avoid many potential problems.

> Mike was talked into having a party while his parents were away for the evening. His friends said that they would help clear up and that his parents would 'never know'. Though he felt uncomfortable, Mike agreed because he wanted to be part of the group. Everything went well until a neighbourhood group of troublemakers gate-crashed. Mike knew immediately he should get help, but thought that by handling the situation himself he could avoid getting into difficulty with his parents.
>
> The troublemakers began to beat the boys, molest some of the girls and wreck the house. Only then did one of the boys telephone the police, ignoring

the protesting host, who said that his parents would 'kill him' for allowing the party to take place. Had Mike trusted his judgement and refused to have the party, none of this would have happened.

For young people, or indeed anyone, trusting feelings includes taking action if they feel they are being followed. If this seems to be happening, they should immediately walk towards a place with people, like a shop or play area in a park. If there are houses nearby, they should go up to the door of one and either pretend to ring the bell or ring the bell if the person continues to follow. They should have no hesitation in picking up a rock and breaking a window if this is necessary to get help. A broken window can always be fixed and it does bring attention! Young people need to know that parents will support them should this kind of situation arise.

Being aware of the behaviour of others

If someone is acting in an inappropriate way, it is best to keep a safe distance. Tell teenagers not to get involved if, for example, a person in the group is making inappropriate jokes or comments, drinking too much, or not listening and offending others. If another person acts in an overfamiliar way, gets too close in a way that makes them uncomfortable, or begins touching them, teenagers need to know that they should say no forcefully and get help.

Avoiding unnecessary risks: hitchhiking

Given the fact that people can be raped, sexually assaulted, robbed, or murdered when hitchhiking, the only sensible advice is: Don't Do It.

Saying no and meaning it

One of the most commonly held myths is that when a girl says no, she means yes (see the true/false questionnaire on p. 171–179). To avoid any misunderstanding, girls should be told to look the person in the eye and say no in a loud, firm voice. They should make sure their body language conveys the same message. Teenage girls should remember that they have the right to say no and that kissing and cuddling should not be regarded as an open invitation to have sexual intercourse.

Becoming angry

In a dangerous situation, many people become frozen with fear and cannot think. Anger helps to focus energy and convert thoughts into action. Tell teenagers to think 'I don't deserve this' and use whatever force is necessary to get out of the difficulty. Teenagers should realise that by acting quickly and decisively, they may be saving themselves from potential harm.

> Jenny had been jogging in the park, wearing her Walkman, and failed to hear the older teenage boy who approached from behind and dragged her to a secluded area. She saw people walking by, but they could not see her. She was terrified and could not remember anything from the self-defence class she was taking. However, when the boy tried to pull down her shorts, she became angry. I haven't done anything to him, she thought. He has no right to do this to me! With that, she yelled a deep, loud scream, pushed him hard and ran away towards the path. He was startled and ran in another direction. Jenny later remarked that her anger gave her strength she didn't know she had.

The Walkman, incidentally, is one hazard that parents did not have to contend with as teenagers - there are some

advantages in growing older! But teens should be made
aware that it is not just their possible future lack of hearing
that is of concern. Wearing a Walkman might suggest to
an attacker that the person will not be aware of what
is happening. As in Jenny's case, it could have harmful
consequences.

Learning self-defence

Taking a self-defence course is a good idea for those who
are willing to do the necessary work and practise what they
have been taught. For most teenagers or adults, knowing and
practising three or four techniques would be more helpful
than having so much information that it is all forgotten in a
crisis. Learning how to get out of a hold, where the pressure
points are on the body, and how to kick, bite or hit to get
away would be useful information for most people. Check
what courses there are in your local area (see p. 155).

Telling a trusted adult

If a teenager is raped or molested, he or she often does
not tell, fearing censure by friends, humiliation or disbelief.
Teenagers need a network of trusted adults to whom they
can turn. Parents can help teenagers work out a list or
teenagers can do it on their own. They should be told to
keep telling until they receive help. Adults, too, must learn
to give help without censure. One enlightened father has told
all of his children that if they ever get into a situation they
cannot handle, they can telephone him and he will pick
them up, no questions asked.

Knowing that the offender is responsible

This is an important message because most teenagers will
not tell parents if they are attacked for fear that they will be
blamed. They may also blame themselves, as many victims of
assault do: 'I did not follow the rules, so this is my fault.'

Parents and others who deal with teenagers should emphasise that it is the offender's fault.

The facts about sexual abuse

Since many people are misinformed about the realities of sexual abuse, discussing facts will lead to a better understanding of the problems. If boys and girls examine the issue together so that the message is the same for both, then they can begin to understand what to expect from each other and communicate in an open and honest way.

The questionnaires on p. 165–179 can be used to introduce the subject. Although the majority of answers are straightforward, the questionnaires should be used to stimulate discussion and not as an exam with 'right' and 'wrong' answers. In the questionnaire for younger teenagers, for example, the answer to question 11 about never fighting back could be true or false depending upon the circumstances.

Teenagers should be given the opportunity to discuss the answers with friends, parents or school personnel such as teachers, school nurses or health visitors. (See also Tips for Teenagers When Looking for Part-time Jobs, p. 138–140).

How teachers and other adults can help

With the increase in concern about children's safety, teachers and other adults who work with children are asking how they can help. Teaching personal safety covers a wide range of problems, from getting lost to being bullied, to being approached by someone who is intent on harm, whether it is a stranger or someone known to the child. The lessons can be fun and children often enjoy them.

Before talking to children about personal safety, it is essential to enlist the support of parents and other people in the community, for several reasons. Community sensitivities must be taken into account, and classroom discussions must be kept within guidelines that are acceptable to parents and the school. There are many components in teaching children how to keep safe, and it is not always necessary to include every one of them. For example, there may be some religious or cultural objections to children trying to defend themselves in a physical way against an attacker. Another important factor is that talking about good touches and bad touches could lead to a child disclosing that abuse has already occurred. If that happens, the teacher will need to draw on the backup network of community services for support.

Many of the ideas at the beginning of this book can be used in schools, nurseries, play associations and youth groups. The following ideas for specific age groups are included here as suggestions for some additional ways to work with children. (For more detailed information about introducing a comprehensive programme into schools, contact Kidscape.)

PRE-SCHOOL CHILDREN

One way that has worked quite well with young children is to introduce the topic of safety by explaining that keeping safe means taking care. Ask them to think up ways of taking care of themselves. Their ideas may include:

• Washing hair

• Brushing teeth

• Taking baths

• Eating

• Drinking

• Going to the toilet

Talking about pets in another good way to bring up the concept of taking care of someone or something. Ask your children to tell you about a toy or something special like a favourite blanket that belongs to them. Use this as a way to explain that their bodies are also special and belong to them.

Discuss touching and some of the other ideas mentioned earlier in this book. Tickling is a good way to bring up the subject of touching as most young children can understand 'liking or not liking' tickling.

Have children make a hug list. This can be done verbally with very young children by asking them from whom they like hugs and kisses. Grannies come top of most lists, with Mummy, Daddy and Grandpa closely following. Four-year-old James declared that he liked his dog's 'lick hugs'. Children can be encouraged to draw pictures or paste up photos on some paper for their hug list.

Brought up occasionally, these conversations with children begin to help them with the concept of trusting their own feelings about what they do and don't like.

Use stories like *The Tale of Peter Rabbit* to introduce the idea that children should tell, even if they have broken a family rule. Peter broke the family rule about invading Mr McGregor's garden and was almost made into rabbit pie, like his father. He did not tell his mother how he had lost his coat because he should not have been in the garden in the first place. In addition, the concept of self-reliance can be introduced by explaining how Peter used his wits to escape from the garden.

Use puppets or dolls to portray what happens in a play-ground, such as one child taking away a toy from another. Ask the children what they would do, how they would help each other and how they would get adult assistance.

PRIMARY-SCHOOL CHILDREN

Here is one method by which children can be taught to protect themselves. Most children have had the experience of being confronted by a bully. The teacher or worker can introduce the subject of bullying by using an example such as:

John is playing in the park when an older, bigger boy approaches and demands John's pocket money. John gives the bully his money and is therefore unsuccessful in defending himself.

Then discuss how John felt, how the bully felt and explain that John had his right to be safe taken away. Ask the children what they would do in this situation. Be prepared for the children wanting to punch the bully on the nose and ask if that would solve the problem: 'Wouldn't the bully then hit back?' Ask the children about telling an adult and if that would mean they were telling tales, as discussed in the first part of this book. If none of the children mentions taking a friend along, suggest that having a friend, brother or sister helping to say no makes people feel stronger.

If the question of the bully having a weapon is raised, explain it is far better to give the bully the money, but that they should definitely tell an adult what happened.

By using the problem of bullies to illustrate the concept of personal safety, the teacher or worker has made the idea of the right to be safe clear to the children.

YOUNG TEENAGERS

Having begun the discussion by talking about rights, give the questionnaire on p. 165–167 to the children (see p. 45 for information on how to use the questionnaire). Do not collect the papers; instead, discuss the answers, which will take at least half an hour. Continue by either telling or eliciting stories of bullies and strangers, and encourage the children to talk about how they would cope in various situations. What to do if approached by a known adult can be introduced when the children are ready. One way this can be done is by using a story about a girl (or boy) who has been babysitting for an aunt and uncle. When the uncle takes the babysitter home, he tries to kiss her and she rebuffs him. The uncle then tells her that the incident must be kept a secret. Discussion should focus on the issues of secrecy and who to tell.

OLDER TEENAGERS

Use the questionnaire on p. 171–173 and discuss the answers. (See p. 45 for guidance on how to use the questionnaire.) Do not collect the papers. Relate the story on p. 40 about Susan and ask the children who was at fault. This can lead to further discussion about responsibility and guilt, trusting feelings, setting limits and the other topics mentioned in Helping Teenagers to Protect Themselves (see p. 39–45). The teacher may wish to give lessons in basic self-defence.

REPORTING CASES OF SUSPECTED CHILD ABUSE

Anyone who works with children should be aware of the danger signs and who to contact for help. Concerned adults are advised to contact their local social services for suggestions on the appropriate action to take. The help organisations listed in this book on p. 145–156 are also available to give advice. The dangers signs of abuse listed on p. 54–70 provide teachers or workers with identifiable physical and emotional characteristics they should pay attention to when they suspect child abuse.

Some children will already have been abused, but have not yet told. It is important, therefore, in discussing these issues with children to make sure they are not made to feel guilty. In one workshop, an eleven-year-old girl started crying and later disclosed that she had been sexually assaulted by an older cousin two years previously. She felt guilty for having kept the secret and for not having said no.

When talking with children, say that sometimes children may be placed in a situation in which they cannot say no or get help. Emphasise that this is not their fault, and that children who have survived abuse and not told are very brave, but nevertheless they should try to get help from an adult. If a child reveals having been sexually abused, use the suggestions listed on p. 75–77 to help deal with the disclosure. Promise to do everything in your power to protect the child, but do not promise that what is said will be kept secret.

THE USE OF VIDEOS

There are now many videos for children about keeping safe from sexual abuse. Well-meaning adults may be tempted to use a video to introduce children to the issues.

This method may appear to allow an admittedly difficult subject to be dealt with in a non-threatening way. If video can work as an aid for teaching maths and science, why not for teaching the prevention of sexual abuse?

Teachers who use videos as teaching aids have usually been prepared in the discipline being discussed and use the video to reinforce and/or follow up a lesson, not to introduce the concepts. Since most teachers have no preparation in preventing child sexual abuse, videos should not be used to introduce the ideas to children.

Videos also keep the subject at arm's length. Adults may think that children understand what to do because they have seen a video. But it is extremely difficult to introduce ideas about safe and unsafe touching in the passive medium of video. Children will have a lot of questions to ask and the discussion needs to be continuous and interactive to ensure that children understand the messages. There is no substitute for talking with children, particularly in an area as sensitive as this.

Nevertheless, some videos can be useful as part of a follow-up lesson after children have taken part in an interactive learning process. A video could then be used as a tool, but not the primary means, for continuing the discussion and reinforcing the message of personal safety.

More suggestions for teachers and workers

- Arrange a parents' meeting. Parental involvement and support is essential.

- Discuss how to get help when a child needs adult assistance.

- Teach children that you give them permission to say no in order to keep safe.

- Talk about the difference between safe 'good' secrets and unsafe 'bad' secrets.

- Help children to establish a network of trusted adults.

- Discuss with children the difference between bribes and gifts.

- Help children to learn how to deal with bullies.

- Help children to learn how to deal with approaches not only by strangers but also by people they know who may harm them.

- Keep an incident log in order to ensure that incidents of children being approached by strangers are reported and centrally monitored.

- Be aware of and follow local procedures.

2

DEALING WITH CHILD ABUSE

In cases of abuse, there may be no outward signs or the child or teenager may try desperately to hide the signs out of fear. This often makes it difficult to find out if a child has been abused. Some parents are stunned when they discover that their child has been abused and blame themselves for not realising what was happening. In those cases where a partner or the other parent has been the abuser, it is even more difficult for the child and non-abusing parent.

There are some characteristics commonly shared by children who have been abused that can indicate something is wrong. Whilst we all hope that our own children (or any children) will never be abused in any way, knowing what to look for could help uncover and stop abuse.

Some of the signs and behaviours listed in this section might just be a normal reaction for a child – for example many children might not want to undress for physical education because they are shy or for cultural reasons. However, if that unwillingness is part of a pattern that includes excuses for not going home, fear of the parents being contacted, and bruising, it could indicate that the child is being physically abused at home.

> A mother contacted me because she was terribly worried about her daughter's friend, Debbie, who seemed to live at their house. Debbie was pathetically grateful when she was invited to dinner or to spend

the night. The mother noticed a series of yellow and brown bruises that Debbie always seemed to have. When asked, Debbie explained how clumsy she was and made excuses. One day Debbie came over with two black eyes and a cut lip. She claimed to have fallen over, but the mother felt she'd been beaten. The mother was right – the child had been the victim of long-term abuse. Debbie's abuse was stopped because her friend's mother had the courage to help.

What to look for

Usually it is difficult for children or teenagers to talk about abuse they are suffering, especially sexual abuse. In many cases, the only way to stop it depends on our recognising the signs of abuse and our willingness to try to get help. Often, after a case of child abuse has made tragic headlines, people say that they thought something was wrong, but weren't sure. Perhaps being aware of signs and symptoms, together with our natural instincts, will make people more confident about trying to intervene if a child is being harmed. Some of the signs are on more than one list, as in many cases the child might be subjected to more than one form of abuse.

SEXUAL ABUSE

There are many definitions of child sexual abuse. It is difficult to find one that satisfies everyone. Perhaps the most simple and straightforward definition is:

> Child sexual abuse is the exploitation of a child under the age of sixteen for the sexual pleasure, gratification or profit of an adult or significantly older person.

Sexual abuse can range from indecent exposure and voyeurism, for example spying on a child undressing or bathing, to taking pornographic pictures, touching genitals, attempted intercourse or intercourse, buggery, oral sex, rape, incest, and involving children in sex rings or prostitution. It can consist of a single incident, or events may occur over a number of years.

Outlined below are the signs and symptoms commonly seen in children and teenagers suffering from sexual abuse.

Children under the age of five may:

- Become insecure or cling to parents in a fearful way

- Show extreme fear of a particular person

- Cry hysterically when their nappy is changed

- Become hysterical when clothing is removed, particularly underclothes

- Have some physical signs in the genital area, including the smell of semen, etc.

- Have soreness or bleeding in the throat, anal or genital areas

- Regress to a much younger behavioural pattern

- Behave in a way sexually inappropriate to their age, being obsessed with sexual matters as opposed to showing normal curiosity (see   p. 61–62)

- Stare blankly, seem unhappy, confused, sad

- Become withdrawn, stop eating, have chronic nightmares, begin wetting again when previously dry

- Play out sexual acts in too knowledgeable a way with dolls or other children

- Produce drawings of sex organs such as erect penises

- Stop enjoying activities such as stories or games with other children

Keeping Safe

- Seem to be bothered or worried, but won't tell why, as if keeping a secret

- Change from being happy and active to being withdrawn and fearful

- Repeat obscene words or phrases said by the abuser

- Say repeatedly that they are bad, dirty or wicked

- Become aggressive and hurtful

One mother noticed that her four-year-old child suddenly started exhibiting several of these conditions. She checked into all the possibilities she could think of, but to no avail. Her son was particularly troubled whenever he went to play at their neighbour's flat. He would come home in a bad mood, refuse to eat and go to his room. He muttered to himself that he was dirty and rude.

After some questioning, the mother found out that the lodger had been making her son and her neighbour's child 'play dirty games', which the children were told to keep secret. These children were also told that their mothers would hate them and would send them away if they knew, so they were frightened to tell. It was only by observing the changes in her son that the abuse was stopped.

Children from the age of five to twelve may:

- Hint about secrets they cannot tell

- Say that a friend has a problem

- Ask if you will keep a secret if they tell you something

- Begin lying, stealing, blatantly cheating in the hope of being caught

- Have unexplained sources of money

- Have terrifying dreams

- Start wetting themselves

- Exhibit sudden inexplicable changes in behaviour, such as becoming aggressive or withdrawn

- Stop enjoying previously liked activities, such as music, sports, art, Scouts or Guides, going to summer camp, gym club

- Be reluctant to undress for gym

- Become fearful of or refuse to see certain adults for no apparent reason; dislike a particular babysitter, relative or other adult

- Act in a sexual way inappropriate to their age

- Draw sexually explicit pictures depicting some act of abuse

- Seem to be keeping secret something that is worrying them

- Have urinary infections, bleeding or soreness in the genital or anal areas

- Have soreness or bleeding in the throat

- Have chronic ailments, such as stomach- or headaches

- Take over the parent role at home, seem old beyond their years (if the victim of incest)

- Develop eating disorders such as anorexia or bulimia

- Become severely depressed, even attempt suicide

- Have a poor self-image, self-mutilate

- Continually run away

- Regress to younger behaviour, such as thumb-sucking, surroundingthemselveswithpreviouslydiscardedcuddly toys

- Show discomfort walking

- Say that they are no good, dirty, rotten

- Be wary, watchful

- Repeat obscene words or phrases that may have been said during the abuse

- Attempt to sexually abuse another child

- Talk or write about sexual matters

- Find hundreds of excuses not to go home or to a friend's house after school (places where abuse may be happening)

An eight-year-old girl suddenly became withdrawn and unhappy, refusing to play with any of her friends. She said she was ugly and started pulling out bits of her hair and biting herself. The child's teacher became increasingly concerned and tried talking with her, but the girl refused to talk. The teacher had a conference with her mother and learned that the child was acting the same way at home.

After much discussion, it was discovered that her grandfather had sexually abused the child on a recent visit. It was one incident and it was the only time it had happened to her, but it was subsequently revealed that he had abused three other grandchildren for a number of years. The children had never told anyone as the grandfather had told them that he would go to prison if they did. The child was very badly affected by the abuse and needed counselling over a long period of time.

Young people from the age of thirteen onwards may:

- Be chronically depressed

- Be suicidal

- Use drugs or drink to excess

- Self-mutilate, show self-hatred

- Have unexplained pregnancies

- Experience memory loss

- Become anorexic or bulimic

- Run away frequently

- Be inappropriately seductive

- Be fearful about certain people like relatives or friends

- Assume the role of parent in the house to such an extent that they do all the cooking, cleaning and child-minding and are taking care of everyone's needs except their own

- Not be allowed to go out on dates or have friends round

- Have soreness, bleeding in the genital or anal areas or in the throat

- Find excuses not to go home or to a particular place

- Have recurring nightmares, be afraid of the dark

- Be unable to concentrate, seem to be in a world of their own

- Have a 'friend who has a problem' and then tell about the abuse of the friend

- Have chronic ailments such as stomach and headaches

- Sexually abuse a child, sibling or friend

- Exhibit a sudden change in school/work habits, play truant

- Be withdrawn, isolated or excessively worried

- Have outbursts of anger or irritability

- Be fearful of undressing for gym

- Have unexplained sums of money

Fifteen-year-old Karen had been sexually abused for years by her stepfather. He told her she was his 'special girl', bought her presents and gave her large sums of money. She had the major responsibilities in the house and was never allowed to go out with friends, girls or boys. She was told that if she disclosed the abuse to anyone, the family would fall apart and she would be the cause.

Because the abuse had been long-term, she did not show sudden changes in behaviour, but had exhibited several signs over the years. She had attempted suicide on two occasions, had become anorexic, could not concentrate in school, was often depressed and continually had health problems.

Karen's plight should have been uncovered years previously, given the number of alarming signals. The abuse was only stopped because an alert gym teacher recognised that Karen's symptoms could be indicative of sexual abuse. Unfortunately, Karen's stepfather did not admit to the abuse and her mother turned against her. Although Karen disclosed the abuse, she later retracted. Karen went to live with her grandmother, but she still needs long-term therapy to come to terms with what has happened. Perhaps the outcome would have been better had the abuse been recognised earlier, but we will never know.

It should also be noted that some children and young people who are abused go to great lengths to conceal what is happening and somehow manage not to show any behaviour associated with the abuse.

What about sexual play between children?

It is important when defining sexual abuse to exempt the normal play of children, which often includes exploring their own bodies and those of other children. When the children are within the same age range and are playing doctors and nurses, this is a normal, healthy part of growing up. It may feel good and be sensual, but it is neither sexual in an adult sense, nor abuse.

This play becomes abusive if there is a large age gap between the children, such as a thirteen-year-old 'playing with' a four-year-old, or if a child is being *forced* to participate.

There are times when a child who has been abused may attempt to act out the abuse on another child. In this case, the level of sexual knowledge of the child who initiates the incident is most often totally inappropriate to his or her age, such as a three-year-old accurately trying to enact oral sex on another child. The child who is 'abusing' is in reality a victim who should be referred for help.

There is also growing concern about the possibility of young children imitating what they may have seen on a pornographic video (see p. 124). At this point we cannot discount the possibility that children may try out what they see. However, we have no evidence at this time to support the idea that children who see these videos have understood enough to learn how to try out sexual activities with other children. What we are finding is that young children who react in a sexually inappropriate way that appears abusive have themselves been abused.

What about children being interested in adults' bodies?

Many parents have recounted the occasions when a son or daughter has been fascinated with the mother's breasts, the

father's penis or some other part of their bodies. Sometimes
the child wants to touch or look at various parts of the body
and adults are embarrassed or even shocked. One father
was particularly worried that it might be misinterpreted
as sexual abuse when his three-year-old daughter wanted
to touch his penis in the bath.

Children are quite often interested in adult bodies. Again,
it is a natural part of growing up. This kind of curiosity
should not be threatening to adults, although in the current climate it is an understandable worry. As long as
the child is instigating the questions or the touching in
a way appropriate to the child's age and it is not being
kept a secret, it is not abuse.

If, however, a child tries to enact something totally inappropriate, you should be concerned about where the child
learned the behaviour. For example, in one case a five-year-
old girl began acting seductively in a very adult manner
and attempted to get her parent to fondle her. The child
had been abused by a babysitter, and since in this case
it had felt good, she tried to get her parent to do the
same thing. Clearly, this child's behaviour was cause for
concern. The parent had to set limits (see p. 82) by saying
no to the child's request and had to seek help to find out
what had happened to the child.

But we should not be concerned about children's natural
sensual and sexual development, which includes looking at
their own and other people's bodies. The more open and honest we can be with them when they ask questions, the easier it
will be to help them develop ways to keep safe. It is important
to remember that children are naturally affectionate and seek
the attention of adults. It is when the adult or older teenager
uses the child's affection as an excuse to become sexual that
abuse occurs. This is never the child's fault.

Who are the offenders?

Just as there are no definitions of child sexual abuse that
satisfy everyone, neither is there one simple and satisfactory
explanation about who are the offenders. Most of the information known about child abusers comes from studies done in
prisons. Since relatively few offenders are apprehended, convicted and sent to prison, our knowledge of them is limited.

From records kept of offences, it is known that approximately 95 per cent of reported offenders are men and
this statistic has been consistent in studies throughout the
world. (However, this should not be misinterpreted to say
that most men molest children.)

Less is known about women offenders, though more cases
are coming to light since the publication of articles and
books about the subject of female sexual abuse of children.
It has been accepted that women physically and emotionally abuse and neglect children, but that sexual abuse by
women is rare. Nevertheless, it is important that we keep
our minds open to the realisation that children can and have
been sexually abused by women, or we will be leaving some
children vulnerable to abuse. If a child claims to have been
abused by a woman or exhibits signs of sexual abuse even
though he or she is not in contact with any men, we must
take the danger of abuse seriously and investigate. However,
statistically it would seem that children are at far greater
risk of sexual abuse from men.

There are many ways to describe child abusers. Nicholas
Groth, an expert in treating offenders, has classified them
into two main categories:

- Paedophiles

  People who have always been sexually attracted to
  children and who are not generally interested in sex
  with adults are commonly called paedophiles. Their
  interest in children often begins when they are very
  young teenagers and it is extremely difficult to change
  their behaviour. Many paedophiles believe that it is a

child's right to have sex with adults and say that they love children and would not harm them.

Groth has found that these offenders are usually attracted to little boys. They will go out of their way to become friends with a child and plan the 'seduction' over a long period of time. If the child says no, they will often move on to another child. They also tend to discard a child when the child begins to show signs of physical maturity. Therefore paedophiles are often Peter Pan-type characters, actually not wanting to grow up or be involved with adults. Children are a reflection of their own narcissism.

- Regressed Child Molesters

Regressed child molesters are usually married or involved in a relationship. They have either children of their own or stepchildren, and these children become their primary victims.

Most regressed child molesters have or have had a sexual relationship with another adult. However, during times of stress they cannot cope with this adult relationship and turn to children for unconditional love, nurturing and sex. Once children are caught in this kind of trap, where the offender has power over every aspect of their lives, it is sometimes impossible to escape.

Most of the victims of regressed molesters are girls and they are not discarded on reaching puberty. In fact, since the men are looking for substitute wives, adolescent girls continue to be at risk from the abuse, which has often started when they were quite young.

We know that offenders have abused babies as young as a month old and children right up to the age of sixteen. We also recognise that girls and boys are almost equally at risk. Some offenders abuse girls and boys, some prefer one sex.

Child molesters come from every class, profession, racial and religious background. Some studies have shown that a high percentage of offenders were themselves abused as children. What is not clear is why so many children who have been abused do *not* become offenders. Equally, why do some men become child molesters when they were not abused as children? More information is needed about offenders so that effective treatment programmes can be instigated in the hope of preventing more children from becoming victims

There are several particularly disturbing factors when trying to prevent child sexual abuse. One factor is that child molesters such as paedophiles tend to gravitate towards places, professions and activities that put them into direct contact with children. They usually look and act normally and often hold responsible jobs. They sometimes attach themselves to families, offering to babysit and take the children out.

Unfortunately this means that children can and do come into contact with people who may try to abuse them. It also means that children may not be believed: because the abuser is 'such a nice person', it must be the child who is lying.

Another factor is how difficult it is to stop the confirmed child abuser. Power is often the motivating force behind the actions of child sexual abusers and in many ways the offence is not about sex. But once the offender has begun abusing children, it quickly becomes an addictive tendency. It becomes a source of gratification and the abuser is not inclined to stop. This is why it is so difficult to treat sexual abusers and why they remain a threat to children. Without motivation people do not change their behaviour. Even if they are caught, the risk of reoffending appears to be very high.

Another concern, as several studies show, is that many victims are created by offenders. One long-term American study by Gene Abel from the New York Institute of Psychiatric Medicine shows that child molesters average seventy-three victims before they are caught. Offenders are usually able to avoid detection because they become expert at hiding their deviant behaviour from their families, friends and colleagues and because children are easily coerced into silence by adult authority.

Until we can apprehend the offenders and effectively

change their behaviour, children will continue to be at risk. We must work to change not only the abusers but society's attitudes that encourage their activities. Realistically this will take years, if not centuries. In the meantime, however, we cannot leave children vulnerable to the greater cunning and manipulative powers of these people.

We have to teach children to tell and seek help – it is the only effective method of prevention currently available.

PHYSICAL ABUSE

The signs and symptoms listed below are common to children and teenagers suffering from physical abuse. There may be:

- Unexplained injuries or burns, especially if they are recurrent

- Improbable excuses to explain child's injuries, given by child or adult

- A refusal to discuss injuries by child

- Injuries that are the result of excessive punishment

- A fear of parents being contacted

- Bald patches

- Bruises to 'soft' parts of the body – upper arms, thighs, cheeks – which might have resulted from pinching, biting, or beating. (Bruises to elbows, knees and other 'bony' parts of the body are usually the result of normal childhood bumps and scraps)

- An insistence on keeping arms and legs covered, even in hot weather (unless there is a religious or cultural reason and none of the other signs listed here are displayed)

- A fear of undressing for physical education (unless there are cultural or religious reasons, or the child is very shy)

- A fear of going home

- A fear of medical help or intervention

- Self-destructive tendencies (pulling out hair, self-mutilation, banging head)

- Aggression towards others

- Chronic running away

Twelve-year-old Mark had a series of new and old bruises on the insides of his upper arms. When his teacher mentioned the bruises, Mark immediately said that he was always bumping into things. The teacher knew that it is almost impossible to 'bump into things' and bruise the inside of your arms, although it is possible to accidentally bruise the outside of arms or elbows. His teacher also knew that Mark was the first child at school in the morning and one of the last to leave. Mark's parents only came to the school on rare occasions.

The teacher talked with the headteacher. Mark was not on the Child Protection Register and social services had no knowledge of the family. With advice from the social services, the headteacher rang Mark's parents to ask for a meeting 'because Mark seemed to be a bit bruised' and perhaps he had a coordination problem or was taking a sport and bruising himself. The headteacher did not want Mark's parents to feel she was accusing them of anything. Indeed, she used the 'softly, softly' approach to try to bring about a joint parent–teacher concern for Mark, not a confrontation. If Mark was being beaten, she did not want her request for a meeting to cause him more grief.

Mark's mother came for the meeting and said she hadn't noticed the bruising. The headteacher suggested a school medical, and the mother reluctantly agreed.

The medical examination revealed evidence of other bruising on Mark's back and on his ears. Social services became directly involved, along with the police. It transpired that when his father was drunk he beat Mark, pinched him on his arms and twisted the boy's ears.

Mark's father was charged and convicted. After a short prison sentence, he was put on probation with the provision that he enrol in Alcoholics Anonymous and receive therapy for his problems. The mother was put on probation and went into therapy. For the time being, the family is living together under supervision. Mark is getting help from the educational psychologist and he and his mother have joined Al-Anon and Al-Teen (see Where to Get Help, p. 148).

EMOTIONAL ABUSE

Emotional abuse is often difficult to detect because the abuse is on the inside, in the hearts and minds of the children. Children who are emotionally abused are told in words or actions that they are 'stupid, useless, ugly, unwanted' and are made to feel completely worthless. Love is either withheld or is conditional – the child must do something for the adult in order to be loved, and that love is not reliable. Emotionally abused children are never sure they are loved and cannot count on the constant support most children get from their parents. Children who are sexually and physically abused or neglected are also emotionally abused.

Children or teenagers who are being emotionally abused may:

- Have physical, mental and/or emotional lags in their development

- Overreact to their own mistakes

- Continually self-deprecate

- Fear any new situation

- Self-mutilate

- Exhibit neurotic behaviour, such as rocking, hair-twisting or pulling out hair, finger- or thumb-sucking (beyond the normal age), compulsive washing, etc.

- Respond inappropriately to pain, seeming not to feel severe pain or becoming hysterical over minor pain

- Engage in drug/solvent/alcohol abuse

- Be insecure about most relationships and not know how to make or keep friends

- Be extremely passive or extremely aggressive

- Expect to be disliked

- Expect to be punished

- Be distrustful of adults who try to help or befriend them, or go overboard and become clinging and pathetically grateful for attention

- Find excuses to 'move into' another family, even if it is at times inappropriate

- Blame themselves for everything

Fifteen-year-old Marie spent all her time at Gill's house. In fact, they could not get rid of her. She constantly put herself down and apologised. Marie never knew when to leave and Gill's mother had to ask her to go. Marie was obviously unhappy at home, but blamed herself, saying that she was 'such a trial' to her 'poor mother'. Nothing was done to help Marie, and Gill and her family heard years later that Marie had a severe drug-abuse problem.

NEGLECT

Children and teenagers who are victims of neglect may:

- Be constantly hungry

- Have poor personal hygiene

- Be constantly tired

- Be very shabbily dressed, with dirty, smelly clothes

- Be emaciated

- Be frequently late or not attend school

- Have untreated medical problems

- Be self-destructive

- Have low self-esteem

- Exhibit neurotic behaviour (see also Emotional Abuse above)

- Have no social relationships

- Compulsively steal or scavenge

- Chronically run away

> When five-year-old David started school, it was obvious that there were problems. He came in the same, unwashed clothes and was always hungry. He had a host of problems, medical and social. His family was new to the area, but a check revealed that he was on the Child Protection Register in another authority. Social services were called in and David and his three younger siblings were eventually taken into care.

There have been some horrifying cases of children being left for days in unchanged nappies and having burns from the acid of the urine, of children scavenging for food in rubbish bins, of children being found living in unbelievable squalor, and of children being found dead through neglect. In some of these cases the children were saved by the intervention of kindly neighbours, in others the children were not so lucky (see Act on Your Suspicions on p. 74).

What to do if you suspect abuse

If you are worried that a child is being or has been abused and has not told anyone, before you approach the child make sure that you are prepared should he or she confirm your fears. We naturally always hope that there will be an 'innocent' explanation for the symptoms or behaviour causing the concern, but if this turns out not to be the case, it is essential that you know how to react and what to do next (see What to Do if Abuse Occurs, p. 75–79).

With young children, talk first about 'safe' and 'unsafe' touching and not keeping secrets, as discussed earlier (see p. 27–28). Do this gradually, over a few days if necessary. Try not to communicate your anxieties to the child. When you feel the child is ready, ask directly if someone has touched or hit him or her. Say that the touch might even have felt good, but perhaps the person said not to tell. Don't accuse anyone or make the child feel guilty. The direct approach, made calmly, is important because young children seldom respond to indirect questioning. They often don't understand what is being asked or they try to tell you what they think you want to hear.

If there is a specific physical indication of an assault, point to that part of the body and ask if anyone has touched the child there. Remain calm and do not press the child for information. Let the child tell at his or her own pace.

One mother related that her three-year-old daughter often had vaginal redness after visiting an older cousin's house. The mother did not want to question her daughter because she did not know how to begin and did not want to frighten the child.

After preparing both herself and her daughter to discuss the problem in a calm way, the mother found out that the cousin was sexually assaulting her child. As do most offenders, the cousin denied it when confronted by the child's parents.

Each adult must decide according to the circumstances how to proceed in the best interests of the child. In this case the child was supported and helped at home, and the parents decided not to bring in medical or professional help. They immediately broke off all contact with the cousin, but since their major concern was not to get the child involved in a possible court appearance, they did not contact the police. Other parents in a similar situation might try to have the offender put in prison so as to protect other children and would therefore contact the police.

> An eight-year-old boy became increasingly unhappy about visiting his maths tutor. Because the child did not like maths, his parents thought he was reluctant to study. This was confirmed by the tutor. After several months of increasing tension, during which time the child began to wet his bed and became aggressive and sullen, the father decided to talk to him about his behaviour.
>   The child finally explained that the tutor had been making him play 'secret games' and remove his clothes. When asked why he had not told anyone, the boy said the tutor told him that no one would believe him and that, if questioned, the tutor would say he was lying. The boy was trapped in what seemed to be an impossible situation.

In this case the police were called, the child was believed by his parents and the police, but because of the lack of medical evidence and the tutor's denial, the tutor was not prosecuted. But the abuse did stop and the child was given support. The concern in these cases is that the offender will go on to assault new victims.

> Another parent became worried when her daughter, aged nine, began to have bad dreams, surrounded herself with some previously discarded cuddly toys before going to sleep at night, and suddenly seemed

reluctant to be in the sitting-room in the evenings. The girl was not having any difficulties at school and showed no changes in behaviour outside the home.

After eliminating all other possible causes she could think of, the mother asked her daughter if anyone had been touching her in a way that made her feel unsafe or if anyone had asked her to keep secrets from her mum. The child said no and the mother was greatly relieved. But the behaviour causing concern continued, so the mother continued to ask about it. This went on for a month, until the mother finally said, 'Are you frightened to tell me your secret because you think I might be angry or not love you? Because no matter what the problem is, I promise that I will try to help and that I won't be angry with you or blame you.'

The child finally revealed that the lodger had been interfering with her, but that she thought it was her fault because it did not hurt and even felt good sometimes. She alternately hated him and liked him and did not know what to do.

These feelings make it even more difficult for a child to tell and get help.

In this case the man was arrested, found to have a history of abusing children, and was imprisoned.

Although it is particularly difficult if the abuse is happening within the family, the concerned adult must seek help for the child. When the suspected offender is the child's parent, step-parent, or other close family member, the mother or another adult can use the same method for preparing to talk with the child. Because of the effects that this will have on the child and the family, it may be useful to get professional advice in advance. Several of the help organisations listed on p. 145–156 will listen and make suggestions, on an anonymous basis if requested.

If the child does say that abuse has taken place, the subsequent safety and well-being of the child must be the first consideration. No child should be left alone with a suspected offender.

Talking with teenagers is often more difficult as they have usually experienced adult disbelief and are reluctant to tell for fear of not being believed. They are also much more aware of the consequences of telling, especially if the abuser is either well known to them or within the family. If they have been assaulted by a friend or acquaintance, it may have happened when they were breaking a rule. They are often afraid that they will be punished for the assault and that they will never be allowed to go out again.

Although asking directly can sometimes lead to the disclosure of abuse, most teenagers will choose who they will tell and when. Therefore keeping the lines of communication open and showing that you are ready to listen and not to blame can be very effective in helping teenagers or children to talk.

The long-term effects of abuse on a child's life depend upon the severity and duration of the abuse and how the child is then cared for by family, friends and/or professionals. Some children, especially those blamed and rejected by their families, carry the scars for life and never form loving relationships as adults. Yet children are resilient, and with proper care and support the healing will begin. Children who are supported have a much better chance of coping and eventually establishing stable relationships.

ACT ON YOUR SUSPICIONS

If you suspect that a child is being abused, but you cannot talk to the child, or the child is not in your care, please contact either the police or the social services, or ring the agencies listed on p. 145–156 for advice. Many people are unsure of how to deal with suspected cases of abuse, but it is better to report than to reproach yourself for not having acted when later the child is found severely injured or dead. Too often we hear a neighbour say after a child has been murdered or found starved to death, 'I thought there was a problem. I could hear the child screaming', or 'Poor little thing was always begging for food and no one seemed to look after her'. If children cannot get help for themselves, action from us may be their only chance.

What to do if abuse occurs

Children cannot be supervised twenty-four hours a day. Even by taking all precautions and giving children strategies for staying safe, you cannot guarantee that they will not be harmed. If your child is assaulted it often results in feelings of outrage and helplessness: 'If only I had picked her up from school this wouldn't have happened' or 'If only I had realised why he was acting that way, I could have stopped it from going on.' The ensuing guilt or even the reactions of other people can perpetuate the feeling that somehow you could have prevented the assault.

Since most children do not want to cause pain to someone they love, they may try to protect you. The reaction of the adult will often determine how much the child will tell. A child may just reveal a little of the problem at a time to see what you do. The following suggestions may prove helpful:

- Stay calm. Try not to transmit your anger, shock and embarrassment to your child. Remaining calm will help lessen the effect of the trauma. It will help your child to know you are now in control of a situation he or she could not cope with alone. If you have had a similar experience in childhood, this may be very difficult to do. When seeking professional help for yourself and your child (see below), you may want to talk privately about what happened to you in the past.

- Believe your child. Children rarely lie about abuse unless they are denying it has happened in order to protect someone.

- Reassure your child. Children often feel responsible for or guilty about the incident; emphasise that it is not the child's fault. Tell your child you are glad he or she told you.

- Encourage the child to talk. Question gently and make sure that your child knows that you are supportive. Do not push your child to give you information, but show that you are prepared to listen.

- Report the incident to the authorities. Sometimes this is not an easy decision. The age of the child, the seriousness of the offence and the possible effects of a court case are mentioned by parents as causes for concern when deciding whether to report. The adult must also consider the danger to other children if the offender is allowed to go free. When the abuse is reported, explain to the child that a policeman or -woman, or another professional person, would like to talk with him or her, and that the person's job is to help protect children. Stay with the child during the interview.

- Praise your child for having survived the attack. Explain that he or she had no choice at the time of the offence. Say that you are glad your child survived and that he or she is now safe. This often helps a child to come to terms with the question, 'What did I do wrong?' Later you can talk about how to keep safe in the future and teach preventive skills.

- Seek medical attention if necessary. Explain to your child what the doctor will do and why. Make sure that the doctor is compassionate. Privately ask the doctor to reassure your child that his or her body is all right, despite the incident. Stay with your child during the examination if possible and appropriate.

- Seek help. Professional counselling or self-help groups may help to lessen the traumatic effect of the abuse.

- Try not to change the routine of home or school. During

times of stress this is helpful because it provides a structure to work within and should facilitate the healing process. If the offender is a family member, it must be decided what is in the best interests of the child.

- Reiterate that it is the offender's fault. Never tell your child that what happened was naughty or dirty. If you do, the child will assume that he or she is somehow to blame. Try not to make judgemental statements about the offender, because in some cases the child may have mixed feelings about the person. This is particularly true if the offender is either a member of the child's family or well known to the child. If necessary, say that the person was wrong to have done this or that the person has a problem and needs help. For younger children it might help to explain that the person was naughty or to compare the offence to a burglar taking something that he or she had no right to take.

- Use puppets or dolls. With young children you may want to use toys to help them discuss their feelings. This can also be helpful in teaching them some of the preventive techniques mentioned earlier.

VIOLENT ASSAULTS

It is always difficult to deal with the abuse of a child, but when a child is badly beaten as well as sexually assaulted or raped, the trauma for the child and family can be overwhelming.

'When they allowed me in to see my daughter, I fainted. There was my eleven-year-old with her face so badly beaten that I couldn't even recognise her. She had broken bones and terrible internal injuries and I was helpless to do anything. I wanted to kill the person who had done this. I knew we had almost lost her and I kept going over and over how this could have happened and why. I was furious with myself

and my husband for not protecting her, hated the
man who had done this, and was angry that this had
happened to my child. Our world was shattered.'

In coping with cases like this, some of the suggestions
listed above will be helpful. In addition, the police and
medical authorities will certainly be involved and a full-scale
investigation will be put into motion. In some ways these
actions and the immediate intervention can be helpful as
they provide a structure and give the feeling that 'something
is being done'. However, most families are left to cope with
the after-effects of the assault, often without help.

If the family and child are not offered professional counselling, the parents should approach either the social services
or their GP for the names of counsellors, psychiatrists or
psychologists. Friends can help by listening and not turning
away. When a child is violently assaulted, people sometimes
find it difficult to know what to say, so they say nothing or
pretend nothing has happened.

However, many survivors of child sexual abuse say that
the often well-meaning silence of people around them only
made them feel guilty or ashamed. They were not helped to
express their feelings, which led to them taking responsibility
for what happened. One person who had been raped as a child
said:

'Whenever I tried to talk to my mum, she just cried
and said she was sorry. It frightened me when she
cried, so I stopped talking about it. I wanted her
to hug me and tell me that she loved me and that
I wouldn't always feel so sad. I guess I wanted to
be reassured that my whole life wasn't ruined.'

Talking and listening will help the child come to terms with
what has happened. Sexual assault is rarely forgotten, but
it does not have to ruin a person's life. Give the child time
to talk about his or her feelings by saying that you would
like to listen and help. Allow the child to talk at his or her

own pace, however long it takes. If your child feels angry or fearful, help him or her to express these emotions. This may also help your child to ask questions about what happened.

If the child asks, 'Why did that person do this?', one answer might be that the person had a problem and that it was not the child's fault. Say you are glad that he or she is alive and that you will try to help them get better as fast as possible. Admit that you do not have all the answers. There often are no answers as to why it happened, but continually reassuring the child that you love him or her and that the child was not responsible will help the healing process.

This process can often be lengthy, both for the child and the family. Other children in the family may need extra reassurance as well, as they can feel angry, hurt, fearful or even jealous because of the attention being paid to their sibling.

What next?

If your child is sexually abused and/or violently assaulted, you will need help and support, particularly if the adults in the family blame each other or if they react in different ways. For example, in one family where a child had survived a violent sexual assault, the mother needed time to weep and talk, while the father reacted by becoming very busy. They both resented the way the other dealt with their emotions and were unable to support each other or their child. Deal with your feelings in a way that is comfortable for you, but try not to impose them on others. If you are a single parent, enlist the help of friends or family.

It will take time for the child and other family members to come to terms with what has happened, for there are no magic ways to get through the trauma of a child being sexually abused.

THE AFTER-EFFECTS OF ABUSE

The way that children respond after having been abused varies greatly according to:

- How the abuse is perceived by the child – as painful, worrying, scary, feeling good, horrible, etc.

- The age of the child

- The relationship of the child to the abuser

- The kind of abuse

- The severity and duration of the abuse

- The reactions of those around the child

- The kind of help the child and family receive after the abuse

Children's reactions vary from being withdrawn, angry or sullen to confusion, aggression, guilt, anxiety, or to self-control and seeming indifference.

HOW TO DEAL WITH THE AFTER-EFFECTS

To deal with the after-effects of abuse, most children will need some therapy or counselling. If you are unable to get therapy, expert guidance or any other kind of help for children who have been abused, there are some things that parents and other caring adults can do to help:

- Explain that you will always be willing to listen should the child ever want to talk

- Be reassuring when talking with the child and stress that it wasn't the child's fault. The earlier suggestions on p. 75–77 are still relevant

- Have Plasticine around and use it in play as a possible way for the child to express feelings

- Use drawing too. Try to encourage the child to draw a happy or a sad face and talk about why the face feels that way. This can allow the child to keep a safe distance, but also bring out concerns

- Encourage finger-painting, playing with water and sand, punching bags, pounding nails into wood, and other physical activities that allow pent-up anxiety to escape

- Fun excursions can also be therapeutic

Abused children have often been left powerless and without good feelings about themselves. To help children gain confidence and become more self-assertive:

- Use the 'No' exercise on   p. 26–27
- Praise them for doing something well, perhaps clearing up or setting the table
- Involve them in making decisions, even such minor things as which jumper they want to wear
- Encourage them to experiment and be creative
- Put their work up on the refrigerator or on a wall and comment about how you like it
- Allow them time and space to themselves – don't smother them

If your child expresses bad feelings, don't minimise what is said. For example, a child may say that he or she is dirty or ugly and you might reply that it isn't true. The problem is that it might be true for the child, so reflect how the child is feeling. Instead of denying those feelings, acknowledge them by saying: 'It must be difficult for you to feel that way. Let's talk about it.' This gives the child an opening to get out some of those bad feelings. Certainly tell the child that you don't feel that way.

Since many victims of abuse do not have a sense of their own bodies, do body-awareness exercises like:

- Moving to music

- Drawing self-portraits

- Drawing a full-size outline of the child on lining wall-paper and encouraging the child to colour it in

- Looking at their own baby pictures

- Looking in the mirror and telling what they see

It is important to help your child establish control over any inappropriate behaviour, such as compulsive masturbation in public. Help by being firm about what is acceptable and consult teachers and anyone else who might help to set limits. Explain to your child that although the abuser said the behaviour was all right, the abuser was wrong.

Children may regress to younger behaviour patterns, such as cuddling an old teddy bear or sucking their thumbs. This may be comforting and should be allowed as it may help them come to terms with what has happened.

- Continue to be cuddly with the child, but *only* if the child feels comfortable. Sometimes a child who has been abused withdraws from physical contact. In this case don't force it, but make it clear that you would like a hug or kiss when the child is ready. This might not be easy for the adult who wants to comfort.

- If you are the father or a close male friend of a child who has been sexually abused, the above applies especially. When a child has been abused by a man, the father sometimes becomes reluctant to hug or kiss the child for fear of it 'being harmful' to the child. If you have had a loving relationship and you withdraw, it could prove even more difficult for the child to make a recovery.

- Tell the child that you love and/or like him or her. Children often feel that they are not worth loving after being sexually abused.

- If the victim of the abuse is a boy, he may be worried about how the abuse affects his masculinity. He may think that he is now gay or that he was abused because he looked weak. He will need assurance that it wasn't his fault and that being abused by a man does not 'turn you into a homosexual'. It may help to say that even very strong adult men have experienced this sometimes. The same applies to cases in which a girl is abused by a woman.

- If a boy has been abused by a woman, he will need the same kind of help and assurance that any victim of sexual abuse needs. There has been a tendency to dismiss these cases by saying the boy was 'lucky to be initiated', although the effects can be quite devastating.

- The same applies to gay teenagers who have been sexually abused. They too will be experiencing considerable trauma and be in need of support. There are organisations that can help (see the list of help groups on　p. 145–156) if you feel unable to talk about it.

- Make time for yourself and find support. If you feel enraged, angry, vengeful, guilty, embarrassed or fearful, you need an outlet. Sexual abuse affects not only the child, but the whole family. It is most difficult when the abuser is known or a family member and changes take place in family life. Although the child's interests are the most important consideration, the opportunity to assist the child is greater if the person helping is coping as well as possible.

- If you are still seething about what has happened, try if possible to do something constructive. Join one of the groups that helps others, try to activate a prevention programme in your child's school, write letters to Parliament about the treatment of child victims, join pressure groups to change laws, start a self-help group or anything that you can think will help children and yourself.

- Help your child decide about what to say to friends.
  Sometimes children who are abused tell too many friends
  who do not know how to handle this information. Some
  children are then hurt when their friends misuse their
  confidence.

- If you are the teacher of a child who has been abused,
  many of the above suggestions may be helpful when the
  child returns to class. It is probably helpful to find a
  quiet moment to say you're glad to have the child back
  with you and that you are willing to listen if the child
  wants to talk about anything that is troubling him or
  her. Then try to ensure that the child is reintegrated
  into the class. If you can, arrange a 'time-out' place
  where the child can go if feeling tearful at first. The
  school nurse can be a good ally.

- If the assault is quite well known about, it may be
  necessary to chat with the children before the child
  comes back to class. This obviously depends on the age of
  the children. With young children, it is sometimes enough
  to say that 'Johnny has been hurt or ill and is coming
  back today'. With older children a caution to be helpful
  without being nosy might be in order. With teens, a word
  about realising it could happen to anyone and consider
  how you would like to be treated now could make the
  transition easier. Guidance should be taken from both
  the child and the family or therapist where possible.

- If the abuse is not public knowledge, then nothing should
  be said unless it is at the request and in the best interests
  of the child.

- If you or your child are concerned about AIDS, in
  addition to the concern about sexual abuse, see Chapter 4 for some suggestions and look under Where to
  Get Help (p. 145–156) for organisations that may be
  able to answer your questions.

When helping children overcome the problems related to being sexually abused, it is also important not to try to be a therapist. This could cause more harm than good, however well meaning you are. It is best to be available, listen and help the child express his or her feelings, but to maintain your relationship as a parent, teacher or other caring adult.

Finally, keep trying to get expert help by asking your doctor or paediatrician, the social services or other helping agencies for advice and referrals. Even if there is a waiting list, put your name on it and keep checking until your child and you feel satisfied that everything possible has been done.

3

BULLYING

Bullying causes the most enormous distress to children. Children who are bullied have run away, played truant, become frightened, withdrawn and miserable, and attempted to or succeeded in committing suicide. Their families have suffered, their school work has deteriorated, and their lives have been blighted.

In some extreme cases when a child has been severely bullied, sometimes over a long period, the victim may retaliate by trying to hurt or kill the bully. Then the victim is in trouble. In one case, a fifteen-year-old boy who had been a long-time victim of a gang of bullies brought a knife to school to protect himself. When the bullies attacked, he snapped and stabbed one of the bullies. The bully recovered and the victim was sentenced to six months in custody.

Sometimes victims have been killed, intentionally or accidentally. There have been several cases in which a child has run or ridden on a bicycle into the road to escape from bullies and been killed by a car or van. In one case a six-year-old was prevented by a gang of bullies from using the footpath over the motorway. He attempted to cross the motorway and was hit and killed by a car.

WHAT BULLYING TEACHES PEOPLE

Some people still hold the view that bullying is a natural part of growing up, something children need to go through in order to cope with the rough and tumble of everyday life. What exactly are children taught when this 'bullying-is-good-for-you' view is embraced? The victims learn:

- That they are worthless

- That being gentle and kind is not valued

- That picking on people who are different is acceptable

- That life is about getting the better of someone else who is weaker than you

- That if you can't cope with bullies it's your fault

- That you must conform at all costs

- To self-deprecate

- That they can never win

- That it's wrong to tell

- That they are failures

- To mistrust people

- To lie to cover up the bullying

- To be submissive

- To live with constant fear

Bullies learn:

- To use power over people

- That brute force is better than intelligence

- That no one will stop you if you are aggressive enough, either verbally or physically

- That dealing with situations by using anger and fear works

- That inciting others to become bullies gives you a power base

- To be impatient and intolerant

- That destroying people who are different is acceptable

- That they can force their will on other people

- To control people using fear

- To despise weakness of any kind

- That they have the right to attack anyone weaker than themselves

Bullying is an abuse of power, which we can see repeated in business, government, institutions and in wars. Little bullies grow up to be big bullies and cause untold misery for others.

WHAT IS BULLYING?

Bullying takes many forms. Physical bullying may involve a child being pushed, punched, beaten, kicked, shoved or thumped. Children have also been thrown into rivers and lakes, dunked upside down in toilets, had objects shoved into their bodies, been thrown downstairs, locked in closets, or had plastic bags tied over their heads. The bully or bullies may use weapons. Sometimes the violence is aimed at the victim's belongings: school work is destroyed, glasses are painted with Tipp-Ex, clothes are ripped, bicycles are dented and tyres punctured, excrement is rubbed on books, possessions disappear. In at least three cases, girls have been stripped by gangs – both single-sex and mixed – of bullies. In one case photographs were taken. The girls were completely humiliated and at least one attempted suicide.

Verbal abuse is just as devastating to the victims. Victims are called names (sometimes with sexual connotations), have cruel taunts written about them and left on the chalkboard or on walls, are told that they are ugly and stupid, are laughed at, ostracised, pointed at, are the butt of jokes and are generally abused. One girl who was told that she was smelly and dirty washed herself continuously. Another wrote in her diary before she committed suicide that she 'hated' her life. Verbal bullying is both difficult to cope with and to stop – the bullies say that the victims made it up or that they 'didn't say it that way', or that they didn't write anything. Since there are no obvious bruises, this kind of bullying cannot be proven unless the bullies are caught in the act. This is why it is so insidious.

Any child who is bullied verbally or physically is also emotionally bullied, but some children suffer emotional bullying on its own. Emotional bullying includes pointedly ignoring the victim, sending the victim to Coventry, raising the hopes of the victim with the intention of pulling the rug out from under him or her, and trying to destroy the self-confidence of the victim. One mother rang to tell me about her daughter, aged eleven. The girl had been bullied by an entire class of girls for more than a year. She was a social outcast. Then one day the bullies told her that if she had a birthday party, they would all be her friends and come. The girl was thrilled. She and her mother made a cake, set the table and waited excitedly for the girls to arrive. Of course, the bullies had cruelly planned the whole trick. No one came, and the girl was absolutely distraught.

Bullying can also be racially motivated, with children being targeted solely because they are of a different race. A boy of ten wrote to say that an older boy regularly taunted him and other black children with cries of 'nignog', 'wire-hair' and other unprintable names.

But whatever form the bullying takes, it should be noted that it happens because the bully has a problem, not because the victims deserve to be bullied. If a bully needs a victim or victims, he or she will find a reason to bully. With a few exceptions (see below), the victim is usually just in the wrong place at the wrong time.

WHAT ABOUT THE BULLY?

When trying to understand why children bully, we need to differentiate between those who bully for a short time because of a temporary upset, and chronic bullies whose behaviour is consistently disruptive.

The 'temporary' bully

Divorce, the birth of a sibling, the death of a relative, friend or pet, boredom, frustration, and abuse of some kind are all difficult situations that could lead to a child taking out his or her troubles through bullying. The problem is usually a short-term one, but it causes the victims, parents and teachers considerable worry. A child who was previously a victim may also turn to bullying in an attempt at retaliation.

If you do find out that your child has suddenly become a bully:

- Try to remain calm

- Find out if your child was previously being bullied

- Gently ask your child if anything upsetting has happened. Be sure to say that you won't be angry if she or he tells you the reason; it could be a 'bad' secret and the child might be too frightened to tell

- Try to find out the facts of what has happened. Talk to your child, to the teachers, and to anyone else who might give you information. This could include playground supervisors, dinner staff, the school secretary, and other parents

- If you can find a reason, address the problem immediately. Explain to your child that while you understand the reasons for the bullying, this kind of behaviour is unacceptable. Have your child apologise for what happened and make restitution. This will help eradicate the behaviour

• Keep in close contact with the school to ensure that there is no repeat of the bullying

• Give your child attention and praise for good behaviour. Assure your child that you know she or he is not a bully, but a good person. Do not characterise your child as a bully or it could become a self-fulfilling prophecy

• If you can find no obvious reason for the bullying, put aside time to talk to your child to try to uncover what has caused this uncharacteristic behaviour. Your child may not respond at first, but keep trying. Gently ask about friends, family, school, home, clubs, anything that might give you a clue, but don't turn it into the Spanish Inquisition!

• Don't ignore the bullying, but try not to make a mountain out of a molehill. If the situation is not serious, give it time to sort itself out

• If the bullying behaviour is serious or becomes chronic, get help. Ask the school or your GP to refer you to someone who has expertise with children's problems, such as a child or educational psychologist, a psychiatrist or a qualified counsellor, or contact your local Child Guidance Centre

• Contact the help organisations listed on p. 145–156

The 'chronic' bully

One mother rang our helpline in extreme distress. She had just been to the school to tell them about a bully who had attacked her child, badly injuring him. The teacher and the headteacher said that the bully and his family had been a problem for the school, but they could not do anything because they were afraid that the bully's father would come to school again: 'The last time we talked to the family, the father threatened us. Anyway, the family has so many problems that we can't do anything. Tell your son to avoid the bully or ring the police yourself.' Because the bullying had taken place at school, the mother rightly felt that her son was not being protected and that the bully had managed to get power not only over the children, but over the staff too.

Schools have a duty to stop bullying, but in this case the staff opted out. Of course, the bully himself will be in for a difficult time in life. Chances are that he will end up in prison and that he will continue to cause misery for other people. None of this helps the victims or their families.

Why do children turn out to be chronic bullies? Some are obnoxious kids who are just spoilt rotten at home and self-confidently believe that the world owes them whatever they want, and that no one else has any rights. Others have had difficult upbringings, in which case they often:

- Feel insecure

- Feel inadequate

- Are themselves scapegoats or bullied in their own families

- Are victims of physical, emotional or sexual abuse

- Are not allowed to show feelings

- Feel no sense of self-worth or accomplishment

- Feel they do not fit in

- Feel under pressure to succeed at all costs because their parents only value success, not the child

Bullies can have any combination of these characteristics. What they share is a need to lash out in order to humiliate others and make themselves feel better or important. Children who are nurtured and loved don't feel a need to humiliate others, but children who are not properly nurtured cannot cope with gentleness or with making mistakes, which they see as signs of weakness and therefore threatening, since being exposed as weak and vulnerable is something not tolerated in their families.

The sad fact is that some children are punished or humiliated for things that all children do, such as spilling a drink, wetting the bed, being hungry at the 'wrong' time, putting a jumper on back to front, or falling over and crying when they are hurt. The child in this situation soon learns that it is impossible to do anything right, never to show feelings, that being weak, making mistakes or being vulnerable are not acceptable. The adults around the child gave him or her a clear message: Be strong, humiliate others, and you will survive in this family.

The child therefore comes to deny and hate vulnerability, which is linked with pain and rejection. When this child can find any chink of weakness in someone else, he or she attacks. The reality is that the bully is attacking him- or herself.

Dan Olweus, an eminent Norwegian expert on the subject of bullying, says that there are four main factors in the backgrounds of these bullies:

- Their parents gave them too little love and had negative attitudes towards them

- Their parents tolerated aggressive behaviour and set no clear limits

- They were physically punished and subjected to violent emotional outbursts from their parents

- They had 'hot-headed' temperaments, though this factor was considered less important than the other three

It would seem, therefore, that the way to avoid raising a bully is to love your child, to set limits, to have reasonable expectations, not to allow aggression, not to use physical punishment, to encourage self-esteem by using praise, and to help 'hot-headed' children learn positive ways to control their tempers. The 'spoilt-rotten' bully can be avoided with less indulgence and self-delusion on the part of the parents.

Children who have already become chronic bullies may respond to controls set by others, as they are incapable of setting their own. However, without the support of their parents, they usually reject any attempt to change or to get help, seeing it as too threatening. Schools can also help by making it clear that bullying is not tolerated at school and by setting firm and realistic guidelines and rules. We do bullies no favours by ignoring their behaviour. They need to realise that there are consequences to their actions and to learn constructive ways to behave. If we simply say 'Never mind, we know you have problems', or 'No one is to blame', we only reinforce the idea that they can get away with their behaviour, and that we condone bullying.

Helping the bully to achieve success at something other than bullying can work. One boy was taken under the wing of his woodwork teacher, who helped him to produce beautiful boxes that the teacher prominently displayed and which were much admired. Another bully showed promise in gym and the teacher subtly arranged matches that showed off the child's skills. Still another was lured into acting the role of the tough guy in a school play (the teacher wanted him to play another part, but you can't have everything). The play gave him a feeling of accomplishment as an actor. All these bullies found a new aspect of themselves that they could like and they stopped bullying others.

To change deep-seated bullying behaviour takes time, patience and understanding from the teacher or another adult, and a commitment from the bully (see p. 181–187 for useful books on this subject). Unfortunately, the 'success' that most bullies achieve is by being 'The Bully', and it is the other children who need help to cope with the problem.

The adult bully

Whilst this chapter concentrates on bullying by children and teenagers, some adults also bully children. In the case of adult bullies, the child is even more powerless than when the bully is another child, especially if the bully is the teacher or parent to whom the child would otherwise turn for help.

If you know your child is being subjected to bullying by an adult in your family and you cannot get the adult to stop this behaviour, you may have to choose between helping the child and allowing the bully to have contact with him or her. Of course, you must decide, but keep in mind that the long-term damage caused by the bullying may eventually destroy your child's self-confidence and ability to cope with life.

If your child is being bullied by a member of the school staff, see suggestions later in this chapter under What Can Be Done? (p. 98–101).

WHAT ABOUT THE VICTIMS?

Most children who are victims of bullying are just unfortunate. The bully picks on them because he or she has problems and is looking for a victim. Often these victims are intelligent, gentle, creative individuals from caring families. They are not fighters, nor are they encouraged to be. They are not chosen because they are short, fat, tall, freckled, black, white, wear glasses, talk differently, have red hair or any other physical reason, although that might be the bully's excuse. The bully will find something to highlight, but essentially any victim will do as long as he or she ends up in the bully's power. The object is to humiliate someone else so that the focus is on the victim and not the bully.

Victims are often so intimidated by the bullying that they don't tell anyone what is happening. Children need to be encouraged to tell. Bullying, like child abuse, thrives on secrecy. However, there may be some signs that will alert you to what is happening. Victims of bullying may:

- Be frightened of walking to or from school

- Be unwilling to go to school

- Beg you to drive them to school

- Change their route to school

- Begin doing poorly in their school work

- Come home regularly with clothes or books ruined

- Come home starving because the bully has their dinner money

- Become withdrawn, start stammering

- Attempt or threaten suicide

- Cry themselves to sleep; have nightmares

- Have unexplained bruises, scratches, cuts

- Have possessions or money 'go missing'

- Ask for extra money or begin stealing money (to pay off the bully)

- Refuse to say what is wrong

- Start to bully siblings or other children

- Appear unreasonably angry with parents

- Give improbable excuses for any of the above

If you suspect your child is being bullied, try to find out for sure. It may be worth just coming out and asking your child if she or he is being bullied. But even if the answer is 'No', don't ignore the signs. Tell your child you are concerned and that you want to help and support him or her, whatever the problem is. Take any indications of suicidal behaviour very seriously and seek help (see Where to Get Help on p. 145–156).

Whilst no child ever deserves to be bullied, there are some children who appear to be perpetual victims from the time they start school. This may be because having been bullied initially they think of themselves as victims. Or it may be that they are so sensitive they take everything seriously and are easily hurt. If your child seems to be bullied no matter where he or she goes – different schools, church groups, Girl

Guides, Boy Scouts, playgroups, camp or any gatherings –
try to think about how the child reacts to people. Perhaps
he or she is lacking a sense of humour, or doesn't know
how to talk to people. Perhaps there is an obnoxious habit
that needs to be worked on, such as picking his or her
nose or continually sniffing. Perhaps your child is annoying
other children through not knowing how to share or play
properly. If there is a reason, help your child to change or
his or her life will be miserable. You might try role-playing
with your child to explore how to approach children to play
or how to share toys. Bribe, cajole or do anything in your
power to stop obnoxious habits, short of making matters
worse by hitting or punishing your child. The help you can
give is worth the time and effort. (see p. 181–187 for books
that might be useful.)

Whatever the reason for the child being bullied, work on
ways to help the child get out of the victim role. Remember
that the best victim from the bully's viewpoint is one who will
get upset and react. That is exactly what the bully needs and
wants. A victim who just shrugs off the comments or ignores
the bully completely and walks away is not much fun.

Of course, if the bully is hitting the victim, this is different.
Teaching a child to fight back may work, but usually the
victim is so much weaker it is unlikely that fighting will
solve the problem, and it could make it worse. One boy
who decided to fight back ended up in hospital with multiple
injuries. However, there have also been cases reported to me
where a punch on the nose from the victim actually stopped
the bullying. What must be avoided is making victims feel
that they must fight back or that they are failures. It
is the responsibility of adults to intervene if a child is
being bullied and cannot cope.

WHAT CAN BE DONE?

If anyone, child or adult, is bullying your child, there are
several steps you can take, although hopefully it will not
be necessary to take them all:

- Talk to your child and find out what is happening

- Keep a written record of what has happened, including dates, times, names, places, etc.

- Talk to your child's teacher. If the teacher is the bully, go directly to the headteacher

- Talk to the headteacher, bringing along your spouse or partner or a friend for support

- If you get nowhere, approach the school governors, perhaps starting with the parent governors. Again, bring along someone else and a copy of your written records

- If the bullying continues, especially if the bully is a member of staff, then seriously consider removing your child from the school. A school that does not take the welfare of your child into account is not a good place for him or her to be

- Contact your local education authority and ask to talk to an Educational Welfare Officer. Explain what has happened and ask for support. Get replies in writing, if possible

- Contact your local MP and get an appointment at his or her surgery

- Ask the Secretary of State for Education in writing to use his or her powers under Section 68 and/or 99 of the Education Act 1944, stating your reasons for the complaint

- If nothing else works and you feel you need legal advice, contact your local Citizens' Advice Bureau or the Children's Legal Centre (see Where to Get Help, p. 145–156) and ask them to help you find a solicitor who specialises in educational law

Fortunately most teachers and headteachers want to stop any bullying going on in their schools, so taking these steps is usually not necessary. However, do not hesitate to help your child by going through the entire process if the bullying does not stop. At least your child will know that you completely support him or her and that you find bullying an unacceptable way to behave.

When talking with children about bullying, be sure to say that one of the most important rules about bullying, or any kind of dangerous situation, is that there are some things they should not try to deal with, such as a gang of bullies or a bully with a weapon. Since their own safety is the primary concern, advise that it is not worth getting badly hurt for money or possessions. Sometimes it is better to give the bully what he or she asks for and then get away and tell an adult.

We can help victims by making them feel good about themselves. It is difficult to bully someone who feels confident. Children might feel more sure of themselves if they have prepared strategies for dealing with bullies. Help them practise ways of responding to comments or approaches by bullies. Use the suggestions in Chapter 1 about yelling and running to avoid abduction (see p. 15–20). You could also practise tricks like walking assertively.

One family helped their son by encouraging him to practise walking, which increased his self-confidence. Initially they had the child walking as if frightened, head down and shoulders hunched. They then discussed how it felt inside. 'Scared,' replied the child.

They then had him walking with his head held high, taking long strides and looking straight ahead. Asked what it felt like, the boy said, 'Strong.' It was a simple way of helping him begin to understand how the bully might be looking at him.

It is best to repeat this kind of exercise over weeks, and to involve other family members or friends, giving the child lots of praise. It should not be done if it creates tension of if it becomes a form of bullying to the child. Then it will only make the child feel worse.

Since victims of bullying are often timid, the 'Saying No' exercise on p. 26 is also quite helpful. Expressing anger through the tone of voice can be a confidence booster.

If your child is tied into knots by a difficult situation such as bullying, help him or her get the anger out and express those feelings. Drawing and working with Plasticine are two good ways to do this. For example, it can be therapeutic to make a Plasticine model of the bully and act out inner frustrations. This can lead to more open discussion and help you to develop strategies with your child about how to cope and what to do.

Coping might include getting friends to help, if possible. One little girl practised saying no in front of the mirror for a month, learned to walk in a more assertive way, and her mother arranged for a friend to walk with her to school. When the bully did approach, the girl looked her right in the eye, said, 'Leave me alone' very loudly and firmly, and walked away. The bully started to follow and the girl and her friend turned around and shouted, 'Get away from us.'

In this case, the bully was so startled at being confronted that she left. In another recent case, two eleven-year-old boys were walking home from school when two older youths with knives walked towards them. Since it was not an isolated area and the police station was within sight, the younger boys both gave deep, loud yells and ran round the older youths to the police station. They gave an accurate description and the youths were apprehended.

Again, being with someone else helped them to cope with the situation. When teaching our children to protect themselves from bullying, we must make sure that they do not use aggressive tactics inappropriately and end up becoming bullies themselves. Nor should they place themselves at risk of greater harm if at all possible. In the case of the youths with knives, the boys felt they would be badly hurt if they allowed the youths to get close enough to them. They took the decision to get out of the situation fast because they knew they could get help. They might not have done the same thing had there been no one around. At least both groups of children had options and were not left vulnerable because of a lack of information.

FRIENDS FALLING OUT

It is particularly difficult when a child or young person has been part of a group and the group turns and starts to bully its former member. Sometimes it is one of those temporary phases that often happen in groups, where one or another of the group is out of favour. At other times it becomes a real vendetta, usually led by one of the old gang.

There are some effective ways of stopping this kind of bullying before it goes too far. Anatol Pikas of Sweden has pioneered an approach of 'Common Concern' or 'No Blame'. The idea is to get the bully or bullies to empathise with the feelings of the victim and to change their behaviour accordingly. They are talked with individually, the victim is also talked with individually, and a teacher or another adult tries to get everyone to see how the bullying is hurting the victim and to encourage the bullies to feel sorry for what they have done or said. The Pikas approach can work quite successfully when the victims and bullies have previously had a good relationship, so the basis of empathy exists. It is much more difficult, if not impossible, if the bullies have never felt any kind of empathy for anyone, let alone their victim.

If it is not possible to change the behaviour of the bullying group towards its one-time member, the victim is left with no option but to try to find a new group of friends.

One mum successfully helped her son to break the cycle by inviting a couple of the boys' families around for a barbeque. It broke the group's desire to bully her son. It also eventually led to a parents' group that worked on the general problem of bullying in the neighbourhood. Part of their strategy was to say to their children that it was all right to tell if they were being bullied – that it would not be telling tales.

But if children are to tell, adults must be prepared to try to help, as these parents did. Then bullying becomes unacceptable behaviour within a community and the children feel comfortable supporting one another.

If this kind of community cooperation isn't possible, try asking over one or two of the group that your child wants to become friends with again. Ensure that there is a lot to do and that they have a good time, which will make it much more difficult for the children to want to bully your child. Gradually increase the size of the group so that your home becomes a focal point and somewhere the children want to go. This is extra work for you, but it is usually worth it. Better to spend your energy creating a positive situation than trying to pick up the pieces of a bullied child.

One of the best ways to address bullying is by getting the teacher, the children and parents in the school to make the prevention of bullying a priority. This problem is one dealt with in the Kidscape programmes and some schools have reported that bullying has stopped. This happened because the children learned that bullying was cowardly, and stuck together. The bully was not only left without victims, but in some cases became a positive member of the group.

Although it is not always possible to stop bullying, it is certainly worth trying to change the behaviour of chronic bullies because of the damage done both to themselves and to their victims. In an excellent long-term study of bullies, Dan Olweus found that 60 per cent of boys who were characterised as bullies at the age of twelve had a criminal conviction by the age of twenty-four, and nearly 40 per cent of these bullies had three or four convictions by that age. These are frightening statistics, given that only 10 per cent of the control group had any convictions at all.

At the University of Illinois in the US, a twenty-year study of bullies showed that children who were chronic bullies from a young age were much more likely to be violent as adults, to commit crimes, to batter their wives and children, and to have difficulty with relationships than children who were not bullies.

Although it might not have been only the bullying that caused these problems, it is evident that bullying can and does cause considerable misery. By helping our children develop strategies to cope with the problems now, we may be helping to alleviate more difficult problems in the future.

4

DRUG, SOLVENT AND ALCOHOL ABUSE

Even young children are no longer safe from the horrors of drugs. Many children have been offered drugs at school gates by unscrupulous pushers who are keen to entice future clients, even to the extent of giving the children the drugs free. Next time, the children start paying – and go on paying. This is not a problem that most parents had to face when they were children, and it is a shock to find out that children as young as eight are being sucked into the drug culture.

The unfortunate reality is that practically all children will find themselves in a situation in which they will have to decide what to do about drugs and alcohol. The choices they make are influenced by pressure from friends, their natural curiosity, the availability of drugs and alcohol, conflicting values and information, their own personalities, and a variety of other circumstances.

Taking drugs, for example, may have nothing to do with the adults around them – some children drift into drugs even when parental guidance and example has been as good as humanly possible. Others are influenced into taking drugs, smoking or using alcohol by what they see around them. Certainly, drinking alcohol and smoking are portrayed by the media as being glamorous and sophisticated. The pressures on young people are enormous.

When we advise our children not to drink or take drugs, we hope that they will listen. However, the old adage that children learn more from what they see than what they are told is relevant here. Adults drink to feel good, to celebrate, to compensate, to toast success, to drown sorrows. Adults take medication and pills to feel good, to lose weight, to sleep, to wake up, to keep going, to dull the pain. The message to children and young people is that we can alter, improve or cover up various aspects of life by taking something: there is no need to feel bad – ever.

Some of the drugs and solvents meant to help children fulfil the promise of eternally feeling good are more foreign and frightening to adults than the 'known' drugs such as alcohol, cigarettes or pills. Few parents feel confident about dealing with the perplexing problem of drug abuse by their children when heroin, cocaine, magic mushrooms, glue-sniffing, etc. are involved, sometimes in a deadly mixture with the more familiar ones like alcohol.

What parents can do

• From the time children are very young, be aware of your own attitude towards drugs and alcohol, especially if there are tranquillisers, alcohol, cigarettes, or sedatives freely available in your home.

• Study the facts concerning drugs, solvents and alcohol in order to be a reliable source of information for your child. Contact any of the groups listed in the Where To Get Help section (see p. 145–156). They may be able to tell you about local lectures or groups that meet to discuss the problems of drugs. Also get one of the books or free leaflets listed in the Resources section (see p. 181–187). Some of these excellent publications define, illustrate and clearly explain the kinds of drugs currently available.

This doesn't mean that you have to become a drug or alcohol 'expert'. But knowing what kinds of drugs are available, what they look like, how they are used and what they are called means that a question from your child can be answered by you. If children feel they can ask and receive reliable information from parents, it may reduce their vulnerability to inaccurate or harmful input from friends or drug pushers.

There are so many drugs available that it is impossible for most parents to keep up to date. Crack, ecstasy and other designer drugs, amphetamines, LSD – the list is endless. But just trying to keep up to date with the latest drug crazes and issues through books, newspapers, radio and television will not only help your credibility with your children, it will allow you to be aware of the dangers.

- Keep an adult perspective. Don't feel you have to be on the same level with your children by using slang and acting cool to prove how aware and young you are. Children need an adult point of view; they have enough of the youth viewpoint from friends and peers.

- Don't be afraid to say that using drugs is wrong and to have rules about drugs and alcohol. If children don't feel strong enough to say no on their own, they can use your rules as an 'out' with their friends – 'My mum will kill me if I do that.'

- Get together with other parents and agree on curfews, pocket money, use of the car, and any other guidelines that make it harder for young people to say 'Everyone else does it'.

- Provide or encourage activities for young people such as discos and sports.

- Help your child develop the confidence to say no. Talk about ways to get out of situations, for example being at a party where drugs are offered. Discuss what to do if a friend or pusher is bothering your child to try glue-sniffing or drugs.

- Find out which parents allow alcohol at parties for children below the legal drinking age and don't allow your child to attend these gatherings.

- Keep communications open. It is important that children feel that you are interested in what they are thinking.

Ask their opinions about drugs, but don't turn these talks into a nightly 'Oh no, it's Dad's lecture on drugs' time. Even more importantly, be careful not to hype the whole issue to the point where curiosity is aroused and young people decide to experiment.

• Depending on the age of your child, explain the dangers of contracting the HIV virus (see Chapter 5) and other diseases such as hepatitis B from contaminated needles. Young children need to be warned about picking up discarded syringes because of the possibility of scratching or accidentally stabbing themselves.

• When discussing glue-sniffing, be sure to explain as well as the dangers of inhaling other volatile chemicals such as deodorants, hair sprays, spray polishes, petrol fumes, etc. Younger children may be particularly vulnerable to experimenting with these substances without realising the consequences.

One way to explain these dangers to children from the time they are quite small is to answer their questions in a matter-of-fact manner. For example:

Daphne was helping her six-year-old granddaughter assemble a model when the child remarked on how good the glue smelled. The grandmother replied that it did, but that as well as being useful for sticking things together, glue could also be quite dangerous. As her granddaughter was interested and receptive, they talked briefly about the good and bad aspects of glue and then went on to other topics.

By using the natural curiosity and questions of children, we can establish early on the kind of communication that will allow for non-emotive discussions of the pros and cons of issues without destroying our relationships with our children.

BE AWARE OF THE EFFECTS

There have been several deaths of young people who have either been given or have deliberately taken drugs at parties. One boy of fifteen died after collapsing during a 'rave'. He had either taken the designer-drug ecstasy or someone had slipped it into his drink – perhaps as a joke – without telling him. The combination of drugs and intense activity such as dancing for several hours can lead to dehydration, but young people don't realise the dangers. In a sense it is like playing Russian roulette, but with five bullets in the chamber. The chances are that when taking drugs, especially combinations of drugs and/or alcohol, and then pushing their bodies to the limit, they will harm themselves.

Young people need to know that they should be careful of what they eat or drink in situations like raves where they do not know the other participants. They also need to be aware that it is never a 'joke' to slip someone a drug of any kind, and that it could very easily end in tragedy.

POSSIBLE INDICATORS

Be aware of the signs of drug, solvent and alcohol abuse. The information from the leaflets mentioned in the Resources section (see p. 181–187) will prove useful, but do not use signs like a check list. As in the case of sexual abuse, there may be other explanations for the symptoms. However, it may be a cause for concern if your child:

- Has an inexplicable personality change

- Starts keeping peculiar hours

- Becomes secretive, vague or withdrawn

- Has frequently changing moods

- Begins needing large amounts of money that cannot be adequately explained

- Becomes slovenly in habits or dress

- Stops doing school work

- Drops out of favourite activities

- Becomes irritable, withdrawn, aggressive

- Seems to be alternately drowsy or unable to sleep

- Begins lying, stealing

- Becomes paranoid

- Has slurred or slow speech

- Begins to associate with people who seem to condone drugs

- Uses or leaves lying around drug paraphernalia, such as burnt foil, needles, pipes, books on how to use drugs, tablets, capsules, powders, plastic bags

- Smells of drugs, such as cannabis, hashish

- Has glue on clothing

- Develops red eyes, spots around face, a red nose, jerky movements

Most of these symptoms could have other causes. Teenagers can develop a need for privacy, for making furtive telephone calls or always be in need of more money. But any significant combination of these behaviours and signs, particularly combined with the paraphernalia and with new associates, may indicate a possible drug- or solvent-abuse problem.

In addition to the obvious physical signs of slurred speech, red eyes and the smell of alcohol, some possible indicators of a person becoming an alcoholic are:

- Drinking to escape problems

- Drinking to build self-confidence

- Drinking owing to unhappiness

- Drinking in the morning

- Craving alcohol at a particular time of day

- Drinking alone
- Having the reputation of being a heavy drinker
- Feeling remorseful after drinking
- Experiencing sleep difficulties
- Missing time from school or work
- Losing ambition or efficiency
- Getting into financial difficulties

Many people may occasionally experience some of these problems with alcohol use. However, if a pattern starts to emerge it is a sign that help is needed.

WHAT IF YOU SUSPECT DRUG, SOLVENT OR ALCOHOL ABUSE?

- Try to be calm and not overreact. It may not be what you think.

- If you don't feel confident to raise the issue with your child, seek advice or support. This can be from your family, GP, or one of the groups listed in the Where to Get Help section (see   p. 145–156).

- Think before you decide to drag your child along to someone to teach him or her a lesson. What if it isn't what you think and your child is humiliated for no reason?

- After you have had some time to consider the problem, sit down with your child and perhaps one other person and talk about it.

- Although you may be angry and frightened, try not to take it out on your child. Being judgemental or saying 'How could you do this to me?' could make matters worse.

- If things become really tense and the discussion is getting out of hand, take a break, make a cup of tea or get some fresh air, anything to relieve the pressure and restore some calm.

- Don't automatically assume the guilt. It may have nothing to do with you.

- Decide on what course of action you are going to take: will you contact your GP, the police, a self-help group, the social-services, a drug or alcohol counsellor, or one of the helplines? (For information on some of these groups, see   p. 145–156.)

- In the unlikely event that your child takes an overdose, act immediately to loosen clothing, turn the child on to his or her side to prevent inhalation of vomit, contact the emergency services or your GP, and take to the hospital a sample of whatever your child has used.

As parents we hope that we will never have to deal with drug, solvent or alcohol abuse in our children. However, in our 'modern' world the use of these substances by our children is a potential danger. Knowing more about what our children may have to face could prevent experimentation and curiosity turning into tragedy.

5

AIDS

When my eldest son was eight, there was a nationwide campaign to alert us to the dangers of AIDS (acquired immune deficiency syndrome). He came home one day, having seen a poster about AIDS, and declared, 'I'm not sleeping with my brother any more.' His brother was then five and quite lively, so it came as no surprise that my eldest might wish to rid himself of him. I was rather taken aback, however, when he went on to explain that he didn't want to sleep with anyone except our dog 'because you can die from sleeping with people'. The AIDS poster said something like, 'You can die from sleeping with someone' and my son had taken the message literally. In the next breath, he asked, 'What's ig-rance?' (Which didn't say much for his reading skills at that time.) It seems that another poster he had seen declared that 'You can die from ignorance'.

The campaigns to raise our awareness of AIDS and the dangers of contracting the HIV virus continue and children will hear and see the slogans. The problem is that they may not understand or may misinterpret the messages. Even young people may not completely understand what is being taught in schools or the information they get through leaflets, the media and posters. In fact, many adults are also confused and perhaps alarmed, but most do at least have some understanding about AIDS and how to avoid contracting the human immunodeficiency virus (HIV) that can develop into AIDS.

What is most concerning parents is that children are asking questions or coming home with half-facts and we are expected to help them sort it out. Some children are being frightened by the connection of death, sex and AIDS because they don't know what it all means. Indeed, many parents have not yet explained sex to their children, let alone that certain kinds of sex can lead to death.

Most parents feel that it is wrong for children to link the concept of sex with death, just as it is wrong to link sex with abuse. It could have potentially harmful effects as they get older and start relationships. Equally, as they do begin to have relationships, we do not want them at risk because they aren't aware of the dangers.

Because most children under the age of eleven are not involved in sexual relationships that could lead them to contracting HIV, unless they are victims of abuse, it seems unnecessary to explain explicitly the consequences of AIDS to them at this point. It is important, though, to answer their questions and address their fears. As when discussing drugs, communication about this issue can be low-key (see p. 108).

Older children, however, are actively discovering their own sexuality and how that relates to others. They are therefore making decisions that could affect their lives. It is vital that they are given information to protect themselves. A discussion about HIV and AIDS might provide an opportunity to introduce them to a range of issues to do with health and well-being. For example, abstinence from sex or drugs is one of the most effective ways to dramatically reduce the chances of contracting HIV. However, the reality is that not all young people will follow this advice.

There are several recommendations about how to be better protected from HIV:

• Avoid sexual relationships entirely

• Have sexual relations with only one partner

• Avoid having sex with people who have multiple partners

• Do not use intravenous drugs (see p. 105–112)

- If you do use intravenous drugs, use a new needle for each injection – never share needles

- Practise safer sex, which includes:
  – using lubricated condoms that have a spermicide
  – avoiding oral-genital contact
  (see p. 147 for where to obtain more information)

- Continue to gain accurate information about AIDS and other diseases that may be transmitted by sexual contact (see p. 145–156 for organisations that may prove helpful)

Until there is sufficient well-researched teaching material available for young children, it might be best simply to respond to their questions and concerns, as and when they occur. Much of the media coverage has gone right over the heads of most four- and five-year-old kids. It may not be desirable or necessary, therefore, to try to explain the problem to younger children unless they appear to be interested or express concern.

Teachers and parents report that by the age of six or seven, children are beginning to have questions about AIDS. At these ages children are better able to take on some abstract concepts. But as they often understand more than they can articulate, we must help them to talk. Otherwise they might have fears that will come out in other ways. For example, one child, having seen an advertisement during an AIDS campaign featuring icebergs, began having nightmares about icebergs and death.

Some children will talk or joke about AIDS with adult vocabularies but no real understanding. For example, children may tell smutty jokes they do not really understand about condoms and AIDS. These jokes are one way children express anxiety, so don't become angry or censorious. Find out how much they understand about the subject. Then give them enough information to satisfy their curiosity, but not so much that they are overwhelmed. Curtail your own anxiety or the desire to tell everything.

If a child asks about AIDS, explaining that AIDS is simply one consequence of infection by HIV is probably more than the child needs to know. Although that may be the most correct definition, it may also be far too much information and too confusing. Better to define it as a disease that, at the moment, affects mainly grown-ups and that they may die from it. However, also explain that it is difficult to 'catch' the germ that causes AIDS so the child won't be worried that the grown-ups around him or her will die.

Point out, too, that so far in our country not that many grown-ups have died from it compared with the total population. Also explain that there are hundreds of people around the world working to find a cure and that, hopefully, before the child grows up they will be successful.

If your child asks if children get AIDS, the answer is only in exceptional circumstances. You can explain that some children were given blood transfusions before we knew about AIDS and that some of those children have developed the disease. Assure your child that doctors, scientists and others are working very hard to try to help the children and that very few children have it.

Another concern of children is the babies who are born with the HIV infection. If asked, say that some babies are born to mummies who have AIDS and that sometimes these babies also get AIDS. You might explain that many of the adults who have AIDS were using drugs that they took with infected needles and that they got the disease that way. Since you and your family probably don't use these kinds of drugs, this is another reassuring factor for children.

There is some concern among the medical profession about the dangers of discarded syringes being found by young children. Children should be warned never to pick up syringes because of the possibility that they might stab or scratch themselves. If this should happen, contact your doctor immediately, as children can be given immunisation against hepatitis B. The other worry is that children might contact HIV from discarded needles, but to date there are no reported cases of this happening.

But there is little point in painting a bleak picture to a child who is unlikely at this time to have to deal with AIDS and who is unable to do anything about it anyway. Although you may be quite anxious both about AIDS and about having to answer your child's questions, keep calm and talk in a low-key way. Don't sensationalise or overreact – children may become worried through your own anxiety.

If children ask questions about condoms or anal sex, try to answer. Avoiding the issue just shows that you are anxious, and they will pick up a more inaccurate explanation from the playground. Keep explanations simple and use words that your child will understand.

One parent answered his young daughter's question about a condom by saying that is was something like a little balloon. That was enough information for her, but if children continue to ask more questions then you must decide how much detail to give. Far better to keep answering their questions, though, than to show yourself unwilling to discuss it. Keep going in stages until they have enough information.

Other sensitive questions can be answered in the same manner. Another parent responded to her son's question about anal sex by explaining that it was 'something some grown-ups do with their private parts and bottoms'. He asked no more questions, much to his mother's relief, but that may not be the way you choose to answer. Perhaps your children know about sex or may demand a more detailed reply. Some parents feel comfortable giving a more accurate definition. That decision must be left to you.

Whatever you decide to do, it often helps to talk to your partner or other adults you know before you are either asked these questions or you sit down to explain things to your child. Some adults even practise what they will say beforehand by role-playing the discussion with another adult. This can prove to be quite useful because it will help you to discover just how much you know about AIDS and it should help you to discuss it in a matter-of-fact way with your child.

Be as calm and reassuring as possible rather than emotive or embarrassed. If your child is old enough, do explain the concept of safer sex. If you don't know how to answer a question, say so and tell the child you will try to find out. Explain that AIDS is something we are just learning about and no one knows all the answers. If you would like more information about the issue of AIDS, contact one of the groups listed in the Where to Get Help section (see p. 145–156).

The most important message about AIDS to get across to children, however, is that AIDS has nothing to do with the hugs and kisses they get at home. You may want to say, 'You won't catch anything from our hugs and kisses except some extra love', or something else that is reassuring to them.

AIDS at school

If a child at your child's school has HIV or has developed AIDS, experts say that there is no danger of other children catching the virus during ordinary school activities. There is much more concern that the infected child will be more at risk from childhood diseases such as chickenpox. Do talk to the headteacher or contact the organisations in the Where to Get Help section (see p. 145–156).

Some suggestions for children and young people who are attending school and have the virus are made by the British Medical Association in their booklet on AIDS (see p. 147).

- Children should not take part in blood experiments, such as in biology classes

- They should wear plasters on any cuts

- They should not become involved with mixing blood in the 'blood brother/sister' ritual

- Children or young people should not engage in tattooing or ear-piercing owing to the risk of dirty needles.

AIDS and child sexual abuse

If your child is abused, you and the child may be worried about the possibility of being infected with HIV. Contact your paediatrician or doctor, who will discuss it with you and arrange a test, if this has not already been done. It is unlikely that the child has been infected, but if he or she is concerned, explain that very few children have developed AIDS. Do not, however, dismiss the child's fears; listen and be supportive.

It is very likely that you and your family will need support during this time. If you do not know where to get help contact one of the organisations listed on   p. 145–156 for information, counselling or advice.

6

AMUSEMENT ARCADES AND GAMBLING

Amusement arcades have magnetic attraction for children and young people. They also attract people who may want to abuse or harm children. This is an obvious danger and children need to be warned about the possibility of someone approaching them, offering to pay for a game or asking them to go with the person to another arcade.

Another problem, and one that is much more likely to arise, is the danger of children becoming addicted to gambling through playing fruit machines. In a review of twenty studies of young gamblers, Dr Mark Griffiths found that 66 per cent of adolescents play a fruit machine at some time, and of these, up to 3 per cent – approximately 90,000 adolescents – develop a serious gambling problem.

It is very confusing trying to sort out what children are allowed to do in terms of gambling. Legally, a child of any age can play on an ordinary fruit machine. However, the majority of inland arcades operate a *voluntary* exclusion of those under the age of sixteen. Arcades at the seaside generally only exclude children during school hours, as many of the children who visit seaside arcades are supposed to be on holiday.

The maximum pay-out for fruit machines is low – less than £10 in prizes or tokens. Something that is clearly stated is that it is illegal for a child under the age of sixteen to play anywhere on a jackpot machine that can produce a large cash prize.

It would seem that it is not the issue of children gambling that concerns the industry. The voluntary code is concerned with *where* they gamble, and during what hours.

Whatever the laws and kinds of machines, some parents are becoming increasingly concerned about their children being addicted to playing these machines. Some children are using their dinner money, bus fares and pocket money, while others are even resorting to theft. There have been reports of children missing school and becoming compulsive gamblers. More rare, but of grave concern, are reports of attempted suicides and even of murders because of debts accrued by young people misusing these machines.

WHAT CAN BE DONE?

Warning young people and children about the dangers and the need to be aware of where they go is obvious advice. Beware of buying teens out of trouble should they continually get into debt over gambling. They will never learn about the consequences unless they repay their debts themselves, whether they do so with part of their pocket money every week or they do extra jobs to earn the money. If your child is gambling and building up debts, then it is more than just a 'passing phase'. In fact, this behaviour may be the basis for a gambling addiction that could last a lifetime. The child needs counselling and help to stop (see the Where to Get Help section,   p. 145–156).

Another suggestion is to help try to bring about legislation that can actually protect children. The voluntary code is confusing and some say it is not working. Perhaps the machines should be withdrawn from public places and children under the age of sixteen not allowed access to them under any circumstances.

At the very least, parents need to be aware of the potential problems that these machines can cause some children and young people, and know where they can turn for help should they suspect their child of becoming addicted.

7

VIDEOS AND COMPUTER DISKS

VIOLENT VIDEOS

We all try to protect our children from seeing too much gore and violence on the television or on videos, but sometimes it feels like a losing battle. We may control what children see in our own homes, but then they come home from a friend's house flushed with excitement because they got to watch the very video we have been trying to protect them from. Since we can't keep them home all the time (we need a break from them, too!), it is inevitable that they will eventually see something we disapprove of.

I talked with one of my children after I found out he'd seen a particularly violent video at a friend's sleep-over. The video was full of close-up shots of blood and unnecessarily (in my humble opinion) vile scenes. We discussed the reasons for my objections to such videos and then my son shrugged his shoulders and said: 'Don't take a hyper-spaz, Mum. I know it was play-acting and it's no big deal. I'm not going to turn into a serial killer!'

Children are exposed to much more on-screen violence than we ever were when we were growing up. When they are little, it is easier for us to protect them from seeing and hearing about violence. We just turn off the television and ensure that Walt Disney and other child-oriented videos are what they watch. Then they start going out, and we discover that they have seen the *Killer Gangs of the World – Blood, Brains and Bodies Galore* video at the neighbour's house!

DOES IT MATTER?

As my son said, perhaps we should not 'take a hyper-spaz' (which I interpret to mean: 'Calm down, you old-fashioned mother, you'). I suspect that a child from a loving family where things are talked about and there is a strong sense of right and wrong will survive the occasional viewing of 'bad' videos. But I am equally convinced that a steady diet of nastiness and aggression will produce nasty, aggressive children. If children learn how to act and how to react to the world by the example of adults and what they see and experience around them, then common sense indicates that seeing too much realistic violence is not a good idea. It may desensitise them to violence and may even influence them to use violence. There are many who would disagree, but I think it does matter.

PORNOGRAPHIC VIDEOS

Another area of concern is the availability of pornographic videos. Watching these videos is a form of child abuse and children do need to be protected from them.

> A teacher of nursery-aged children contacted Kidscape to say that some of her children were coming into class too tired to do anything. When questioned, they talked about being up late watching pornographic films on video. When she talked to the parents, she was astounded to discover that they thought the children were 'too young to understand' what was happening on the videos, and that therefore it didn't matter if they saw them.

One young mother wrote to say that she was horrified when she came to collect her three-year-old from the child-minder's to find her child watching an explicit video nasty with the minder's husband. The husband said the children 'weren't bothered' and it kept them quiet. The mother took her child away and reported the matter to the local authority. In a case like this there is concern that the child could be subjected to abuse by the person watching the video. If the child then tells about abuse, the person can use the video as an excuse: 'I might have shown a video, but I never touched the child. The child is just talking about what was on the video.' Children can thus be accused of making up false allegations based on seeing pornographic videos.

What a child cannot describe from having seen such a video is what abuse feels like – the smells, the tastes, the actual feelings. For example, although a child might be able to describe oral sex from seeing a pornographic video, the child would not know that 'it hurt', or that 'something came out that was sticky and white', or that 'I couldn't breathe'. These words come from experiencing the abuse, not from seeing a video.

COMPUTER DISKS

The speed of change in technology means that hard-core and often violent pornography has now become available on computer disks. This allows anyone with a computer to have access to disks that produce very realistic images, including images of violent rape, sadism, paedophilia and bestiality. The difficulty in controlling this kind of perverted software is that it is easily copied, pocket-size, and can be handed from person to person. Parents are worried because there have been cases of these disks being exchanged between children in school playgrounds, and of disks being given to children by adults who may be enticing them into abusive relationships.

The images shown on the computer disks are not cartoon-like pictures, but high-quality photographic reproductions. In fact, famous people are finding that their faces have been superimposed on nude models and that they are being used in pornographic stories. These images can be transmitted with ease throughout the computer world.

WHAT CAN WE DO?

Since the vast majority of homes now have video recorders, it is impossible to ensure that our children will never see an inappropriate film. Also, most children have access to a computer, either at home or at school, allowing them to watch computerised pornography. However, there are some precautions we can take to guard children from both violent and pornographic videos, and from computer pornography:

- Ensure that whoever is taking care of your children does not show them videos you do not approve of. Say something like: 'Jenny has terrible nightmares and I don't want her to see these videos!'

- Deal only with reputable video shops that cater for families. They should be members of the Video Standards Council and/or the Video Trade Association, both of which promote a Code of Practice

- Check what your older children are watching at their friends' houses, if possible

- If you can, agree with other parents not to hire certain videos. This eliminates the 'everyone does it' argument

- Ensure that you and your spouse/partner agree that your children shouldn't see certain types of videos, even if you have disagreement from the children

- Ensure that your video shop knows the ages of your children and will not give them videos for an older age group. If they do, they are breaking the law and could be fined

- Ask your local shop not to stock sexually violent videos. If they won't cooperate, change shops, or at the very least ask that such titles be out of sight on the top shelves or in another room

- Be aware of computer-disk pornography and ensure that your child's school knows about it

- Supervise computer use and acquire a knowledge of how computers work so that you can see what your children have stored on disks

- Teachers and parents need to be alert for pornographic disks being used and traded by children

- Explain to your children why you dislike and disapprove of violent and/or pornographic videos and disks

- If they have been exposed to anything bad, explain that real life isn't like that and talk about how people should relate to each other by being gentle and kind, not nasty and exploitative

- Help your children find a way to say no to seeing inappropriate videos or using pornographic disks – they may end up in a difficult situation and not know how to extract themselves

- Work out a code so that your child can ring you if he or she needs to get out of such a situation. A child could ring and say: 'You told me to ring at four o'clock, but I forgot.' That would be your cue to ring back in a few minutes and say that you want the child to come home or that you are on your way to collect him or her

- Try to watch videos before showing them to children if you have any doubts about their content

- Check the video rating guide posted at your video shop to see if the video is suitable for your children or teenagers

There may be times when you disagree with the rating and want to let your child see a video with an older age rating. There may be times when you mistakenly show a video and wish you hadn't – parents never get it right all the time. The technological revolution continues and heaven knows what we will have to learn to deal with next in this field, but we'll have to cope and do the best we can.

In the meantime, I suggest we scrap the whole lot and go back to reading to our children – much cheaper and better for all as far as I'm concerned!

8

OTHER TIPS FOR SAFETY

When to give independence

Parents are always concerned about when they should first allow children to venture out in pairs or alone. One mother stated that she would permit her children to be independent 'next year'. She said the only problem was that when next year came, it was always too soon.

Having surveyed 4,000 parents over a two-year period about this question of independence, the only thing that everyone agreed on was that the maturity of the child and not his or her age should determine the degree of independence. Where the family lived and the distances children were going to travel were also important factors. However, there was a certain consensus about the age at which most parents:

- Started allowing children to cross local roads. Having reached the maturity level of nine years was the agreed mean age

- Allowed children to go to the cinema or shopping. With a friend or sibling, the average age was twelve

- Permitted children to use public transport for local journeys in daylight hours. It was generally agreed that eleven or twelve was a reasonable age for this

- Allowed young people out on their own or with a friend

during evening hours before eleven p.m. Parents were most concerned about this, but most thought that age fifteen or sixteen was all right

All the parents questioned said that they worried constantly when first giving children independence and continued to worry at least a little no matter how old their children were. One father said that he never slept soundly until his whole brood was in, though the eldest was now twenty-two.

Although it is one of the most difficult tasks for a parent, we must help our children towards being independent. Teaching them strategies for helping themselves should make the task a little easier.

Tips on public places

Children and young people need to be aware of safety strategies to use in a variety of situations.

LIFTS AND STAIRWAYS

Talk with children and teenagers about what they should do if they feel uncomfortable about using either the stairs or a lift if there are people around who worry them. An eight-year-old girl was recently sexually assaulted in a lift when a man got into the lift and stopped it between floors. In this case, the child did exactly as she was told because there was no chance of escape or of attracting anyone's attention by yelling. She survived the attack, though was emotionally damaged. Later she recounted how she had thought of getting out when the man got into the lift, but didn't want to appear rude.

Although it may take them longer to get to their destination, children and teens should always feel they should get out of a lift if they feel at all concerned. Explain that they can either walk out and wait for the lift to return, or get out on another floor if it is safe to do so. The same applies to using the stairs – better to wait a few minutes, or even longer, if there is a person or a group of people who make you feel unsafe. By discussing it, you can help children plan what to do if the situation should arise.

PUBLIC TOILETS

If possible, always go with your child when using a public toilet. As they grow older, however, this becomes problematic. For example, by the age of eight most boys refuse to go into the woman's toilet. This leaves mothers outside shouting, 'Are you all right?' and little boys saying, 'I can take care of myself.' The same applies to fathers taking care of daughters. As parents we are left with no choice and we should therefore encourage children to build up their self-confidence.

Nevertheless, we must also talk with children about what to do if they are accosted in a public toilet. At a meeting about children's safety, one mother told how her nine-year-old son had gone to use the toilet in a very well-known eating place that welcomes children. He came out looking pale and agitated. A man had fondled him and the boy had been too frightened even to run. The mother had not thought about warning her son and certainly did not consider this kind of incident possible in such a place.

Had the boy known that he should have left when the man started talking about showing him a surprise, the assault might not have happened. It is planning strategies with children – 'What would you do if?' type questions – and giving children permission to leave situations that provide the basis of keeping safe.

PUBLIC TRANSPORT

If children and teenagers are travelling on trains or the underground, tell them always to get into carriages where there are other people. If possible, they should travel in the carriage with the guard. Also explain that they should change carriages if they find themselves alone, if there is just one other person or a gang that seems to be together in the carriage.

Make sure that they know about how and when to use the
emergency handle or cord. A teenage boy was beaten by a
gang while travelling in a carriage alone. He considered pulling the emergency cord, but thought he would automatically
have to pay the fine. Another child in a similar situation was
too short to reach the handle and did not think to stand on
the seat. One important point to remember when travelling
on the underground is to pull the emergency handle when
the train is in the station, rather than when it is moving.

When travelling on buses, children should sit downstairs
near the conductor or driver. When travelling by taxi, licensed
taxis should always be used if possible. The driver should be
asked either to escort the child or to wait until he or she is in
the flat or house. When leaving any form of transport, children
need to make sure that they are not being followed. If they feel
uncomfortable, it is best not to leave. Better to stay on for one
more stop, which might be safer than getting off. Tell children
or teens that they can always ring you to collect them or to
take a taxi that you will pay for when they arrive.

A good habit to instil in children from the time they start
going out on their own is always to carry enough money for a
return journey home and never to spend it on anything else.

These same kind of strategies apply to going to the cinema,
to swimming baths, to playgrounds and parks, to dances, to
clubs, and to any other place where children or young people
may find themselves. Of course it is best always to accompany
young children, never to leave them alone in cars or at home,
and generally to ensure their safety. But as children grow,
they must develop ways to cope with being on their own.
Hopefully they will never have to use the strategies mentioned
above, but at least we can give them some options.

Telephone tips

Children should be taught how to use the telephone as it
can be a lifeline to them in case of an emergency. Be sure
that your children know how to use dial, push button and
pay telephones.

Do *not* teach children to answer the telephone by repeating their name and telephone number. Many obscene telephone callers continue to ring back after being told the number they have reached. Since these callers often seem to dial at random, it is best not to give them a way to ring back.

Help children and teenagers practise making an emergency call. Explain that you do not need money to call from a pay telephone if you dial 999 or 100. It is also important for children to know that they can make a reverse-charge call and how to do so.

It is helpful to role-play using a telephone, since during an actual emergency it is difficult to remember what to do if you've only been told and have never done it. In fact, write your telephone number and address in large print by the telephone as people often forget this vital information when making a call under stress.

Explain that the operator will want to know your telephone number and which service you need – fire, police or ambulance. The service will also ask for your name, address and the location of the emergency. Depending on the age of your child, this is probably the only circumstance under which it is all right to give out a name, address and number over the telephone.

Make your child pretend to dial 999 to report a fire.

Acting as the operator, say:

Adult: 'Emergency, what is your number?'

Child: '800 6543.'

Adult: 'Which service do you want?'

Child: 'Fire.'

Adult: 'Fire Service, what is your number?'

Child: '800 6543.'

Adult: 'Your name?'

Child: 'John Smith.'

Adult: 'Where are you calling from?'

Child: '42 Meadow Grove.'

Adult: 'What is the emergency?'

Child: 'The house next door is on fire.'

Practise several times over a week, using different services. After the child is comfortable with the idea, try making it a surprise game to ensure that your child automatically knows what to do. You might set a problem such as: 'There's been an accident involving a car and a motorbike. You're the only witness. What do you do?' Reward the correct responses. As emergencies arise unexpectedly, it is a good idea to be able to respond quickly.

The exchange with the emergency services usually takes less than a minute, although it may seem quite time-consuming. Impress on children that they should try to get an adult to make emergency telephone calls if possible, and that *no one* should make one unless there really is an emergency.

OBSCENE CALLS

Explain that some people don't use the telephone correctly and it is possible that a person could ring up and say something rude or even just breathe in a funny way. Some suggested advice to your child might be:

> Hang up immediately. What the caller wants you to do is to react to what is being said and he or she will probably not ring again if there is no reaction. If the person rings back and there is no one home to help you deal with the situation, try to ring for help from a grown-up. This can be your parents, grandparents or a neighbour. If this is not possible, take the telephone off the hook until an adult gets home and immediately tell what happened.

Getting an obscene telephone call can be a frightening experience for anyone. Acknowledge that it is frightening and encourage the child to talk about his or her feelings. Try not to dismiss a child's questions such as 'Will that person come and find me?' This is a real worry and saying 'Of course not' might not help. One way to deal with this kind of question is: 'You must be worried about that. What did he say would happen?

Allow the child to respond and talk through some of his or her concerns. Explain that the people who make these kinds of telephone calls have problems, but that they hide at home and do not come after people. Assure the child that the person cannot see him or her and does not know where you live. If your child has bad dreams after such a call, see p. 39.

If the calls persist, contact the police or have your calls intercepted by the operator. In one case, the child was more reassured by the arrival of the police than anything her mum had said. The reality that it is difficult to apprehend the culprit was not important – the police officer made the child feel more protected and she felt that something was being done.

A further alternative is to keep a whistle next to the telephone and after ensuring that it is the obscene caller, blast away. Finally, if the calls cannot be stopped in any other way, have your number changed (see p. 155).

TAKING MESSAGES

If your children answer the telephone when at home alone, explain that they should never admit to being alone (see also Babysitting below). Practise answers such as 'My mum is in the bath. If you will leave your number, she will ring you back', or 'My dad is having a nap, may I take a message please?' The friends of one child's mum were amazed at the number of baths she seemed to take, so do vary the message from time to time.

TELEPHONE HELPLINES

The number of children and young people who feel the need to talk about a wide range of issues has become apparent from how many of them ring ChildLine, the NSPCC, the Samaritans, Kidscape and other telephone helplines. Although we may feel that it is preferable for children and teens to talk about their concerns with someone they know, this is not always possible. In some cases, where a child is being beaten or otherwise abused at home, the child may feel it is impossible to tell anyone else.

Alternatively, a child may just want to discuss a problem, such as being pressured to take drugs or being bullied, with someone from outside the family. These telephone listening services can provide a valuable source of advice and comfort to some children and young people. The long and successful history of the Samaritans with adults and young people attests to this.

The helplines can also act as an interim step in getting children to seek help in bullying and abusive situations. ChildLine and Kidscape receive thousands of calls from children who are being bullied or abused and feel they have nowhere to turn.

Although we want our children to talk with us, it is a good idea to make them aware that they have the option of talking with helplines, other members of the family or friends. Children and young people often need someone besides Mum or Dad to listen to their concerns.

TELEPHONE INFORMATION SERVICES

Telephone information services are usually pre-recorded messages that you can ring to find out about horoscopes, sports, travel information and competitions, and also to sort out sexual and other problems. The numbers are sometimes given at the end of advice columns in newspapers and magazines. Some of the information may not be what you would wish your eight-year-old to listen to, such as 'How to Reach a

Climax' or 'How to Deal with Impotency'. Parents cannot be all-knowing or hover around the telephone, but we can look over our telephone bills (these calls are charged at premium rates) to see if any of these numbers are being called. At the very least, we all need to be aware that these messages, which may have some value for adults, are also available to any child who can use the telephone.

There are also one-to-one telephone services available that require a pin number. With this service you talk to someone who might read you your tarot cards or engage in 'non-offensive sex conversations'. As a pin number is needed, it is unlikely that children will be using this 'service'.

It is possible to complain about or block these services by contacting British Telecom (see Where to Get Help, p. 155).

Tips on babysitters

Finding a babysitter is not always easy, but parents need to consider carefully any person who is left in charge of their children. Unfortunately, molesters do sometimes advertise themselves as babysitters as it is an excellent way to make sure that children are on their own. Therefore, when choosing a babysitter try to:

• Find a trusted family member or friend with whom you and your child feel comfortable and happy

• Find babysitters who have been recommended by friends, but do check references

• Make arrangements with friends to babysit for each other's children

• If you must use a stranger, check several references

• Be very aware of your child's reaction when you say that the babysitter is coming. One little girl cried and cried whenever she was left with the lodger. Her mum thought it was temper, though she wasn't like that with anyone else. The child was scolded for her behaviour. The lodger, a trusted individual, abused her over a two-year period

- Ring home to check and ask to speak to your child. This is another situation in which a codeword might be useful so that the child can signal concern. Explain to your child that you will come home if he or she uses the codeword, but that it should be used *only* if the child feels in danger. Otherwise, you could end up coming home just because the TV is broken!

- Be concerned if the babysitter makes excuses so that you cannot talk with your child

- Be wary of men who always make a point of volunteering to sit and seem much more interested in your child's friendship than your own. These same people may continually offer to take the children out to give you a break. This does not mean to mistrust all men or not to let them babysit! However, this particular pattern of only being interested in children could be a warning sign

- Always provide the babysitter with emergency telephone numbers and other contacts. If you don't have a telephone, make sure that the sitter knows where to find the nearest one

Tips for teenagers when looking for part-time jobs

When deciding on a job, working a paper round or babysitting for anyone, it is important to be aware of who you are working for and what to do in emergencies:

- Don't answer adverts that ask for sitters or other casual jobs when on your own. One fifteen-year-old recently responded to a card in the newsagent's and arranged to meet the 'father' at a place that turned out to be a derelict house. She was raped and beaten. The offender was not found

- Accept jobs through friends, if possible, and find out about the people in advance. Go along with your friend or a parent to meet the employer before accepting the position

- Be sure that your parents know where you are and how to contact you

- Find out about how you will get to the job and back home. If it is late, arrange a ride with your parents or the child's parents if babysitting

- If the person who is supposed to give you a lift is drunk, under no circumstances go with them. Phone your parents, a friend or a taxi. A job is not worth your life

- If babysitting, know where to contact the children's parents

- Don't let anyone know that you are alone, whatever the job. If someone rings to talk to your employers, just say they aren't available at the moment. Make up an excuse like 'They are taking stock, can I take your number?' or 'The children's father is resting at the moment, can I get him to return your call?'

- If something happens that frightens you, do not hesitate to ring for help, either from your parents or from the police

- If babysitting do not answer the door or allow the children to unless you have previous arrangements with someone who is coming with the knowledge of the parents

- Be aware of how to make an emergency telephone call (see p. 132–4)

- Find the quickest ways out of your place of employment

in case of fire or other emergencies. If babysitting, plan in advance how you would get the children out with you

- If you do a paper round, be aware if someone seems to be acting suspiciously or appears to be following you. If you have even the slightest doubt, knock on the door of one of your customers or go into the nearest shop. It does not matter what time it is, early morning or late at night – get someone's attention

- If you need urgent help or are frightened for your safety in whatever job you are doing, do not be afraid to make a fuss or break a window to call attention to the situation

- Always report anything like being followed, flashed at or seeing someone who appears to be in difficulty, no matter how insignificant it may seem to you. Reporting an incident could alert the police to a real danger and might even save a life. In many of the reports of children and young people who have gone missing, witnesses have often come forward after the event to tell of suspicious people who were around just before the child disappeared. By being alert and telling someone, you might be able to help prevent a child being harmed

- Also be aware of and report any incident relating to property, for example a smashed window, that could be a sign of vandalism or burglary. But do not investigate it or you might be placing yourself at risk

9

CONCLUSION

Does prevention work?

The positive message of this book is that parents and adults who care about children and young people do have ways of helping them learn how to stay safe. Despite the disturbing facts about sexual abuse, the worries about drug, alcohol and solvent abuse, the concern about bullying and other problems, there are many reported incidents of the effectiveness of teaching prevention. Of course, in the examples below it is not possible to know if children would have reacted in the following ways without being taught. However, the children reported that they knew what to do because they had thought about and practised ways to keep safe.

Below are just a few of the hundreds of cases reported to Kidscape.

• Twelve-year-old Jane and her nine-year-old brother Edward were walking through a large common area when two teenage bullies tried to attack them. Both children started shouting for help, kicked the attackers and made a general commotion. The teenagers ran away and the children went for help, contacting their parents, who telephoned the police. The children were both shaken, but unhurt.

• One nine-year-old girl was in a community-centre toilet

when a stranger tried to grab her. She responded with a loud yell and kicked him hard on the shin. This startled him long enough for her to run out and get help. The man fled with staff in pursuit, but got away. The child was safe.

- A teenager was at a party where alcohol and drugs were offered. There was strong pressure to join in, but the girl excused herself to 'go to the loo'. She then telephoned her parents and arranged for them to collect her.

- After a workshop, a seven-year-old boy revealed that a neighbour had touched him in his private parts the previous week. The child had been told that this was a 'special secret' not to be told to anyone. The parents were contacted, the family given supportive help and the offender was arrested. The child was saved from further molestation and seems to be recovering because of the way in which the situation was handled. He was believed, told that it was not his fault and praised for telling.

- A fifteen-year-old boy, Tony, was at a party with friends when a group of older boys gate-crashed. They turned over the furniture, broke glasses and started becoming abusive to the girls. The teenagers were frightened and there were no adults around. Tony edged away and left the party by a back entrance, went to the nearest telephone and rang for the police. He was scared, but later said that discussing 'What if?' situations at home had helped him remain calm and plan what to do.

- Three weeks after a workshop, an eight-year-old girl told her teacher that her fifteen-year-old brother was coming into the bathroom while she was bathing and trying to touch her. The girl told him to leave her alone and with the help of the teacher told her mother. The abuse was stopped before it started and the boy received counselling.

- Twelve-year-old Emily was offered a drug by one of the older students at her school. She felt too frightened to say no because she was on her own and the older student threatened her. Emily pretended to go along and accept the drug. She even promised not to tell because she was worried about being hit. As soon as she got away, she told the school nurse. Emily understood that her safety was worth the pretence and that she was not bound by her promise.

• A fourteen-year-old girl told her mother that her step-father was coming into her bedroom at night and trying to kiss and fondle her. Although at first the mother did not believe her, the school social worker helped the mother to understand that the girl was telling the truth. The family received help from the social services.

• Eleven-year-old Sharon was walking home after school when a man in a car called to her. She kept her distance and ran into a shop. She noted the kind of car and was able to give a description of it and the man to the police.

• A teenage girl had been babysitting. When the father of the children offered to take her home, she was quite worried because he had obviously had too much to drink. She politely told him that she had rung her parents earlier in the evening and they were planning on collecting her (not true). The man insisted that he would drive her, so the girl asked to ring her parents to explain. She and her parents had a pre-arranged code to indicate trouble. The girl used the code and because they had previously discussed various possible difficulties, the parents were able to figure out the problem. They told her not to leave under any circumstances and came over immediately.

• A ten-year-old boy was approached by a gym instructor who tried to fondle him. He said no and told his parents. Two other cases were uncovered and the police were called in.

• A babysitter offered a six-year-old child a sweet to take

off his clothes and play 'secret' games. The child put himself to bed and told his parents when they came home.

- A young teenage girl met an older boy at a disco. He bought her drinks and offered to take her home to 'meet his parents'. She felt very grown-up and agreed to go with him. He seemed very nice, though he was, in her words, 'a little drunk'. When they got to his flat, his parents weren't there and she started to get worried. He began kissing her and acting aggressively. Although she was frightened, she acted calmly and started talking in a reassuring and friendly way. She asked for a drink and when the boy went into the kitchen, she ran out of the front door and knocked loudly on the door of another flat on the floor below. Luckily, the people answered and she was able to ring for help.

It is unrealistic to think that children can always keep themselves safe, but in these cases the children were able to say no and get help. We will never know whether these and the other children we have heard about would have kept safe anyway. How do you assess what might have happened but didn't? But it does seem that learning preventive techniques helps children know what to do in dangerous situations, and makes them more confident and less vulnerable.

By educating children about practical ways of avoiding dangerous situations and teaching them that it is all right to say no, to get away, to seek adult help and not to keep bad secrets, we are permitting them to use their judgement to protect themselves.

All children have the right to be safe. It is the responsibility of adults to protect this right.

10

WHERE TO GET HELP

The following agencies and organisations can listen and give you advice about a variety of problems and concerns. Of course, you can always contact the police, social services and your GP. Someone in your religious community may also be able to help. When contacting any of the listed organisations, you will need to use your own judgement about the suitability of their service or advice for your particular needs.

Abduction (parental)

The Child Abduction Unit, The Lord Chancellor's Department, 81 Chancery Lane, London WC2A 1DD, tel. (071) 911 7045/7047/7094
If your child has been abducted from the UK, the Child Abduction Unit will give advice about what action you can take and what the British Government can or cannot do to help.

Reunite, National Council for Abducted Children, PO Box 4, London WC1X 8XY, tel. (071) 404 8356
A booklet entitled 'Child Abduction' is available from Reunite.

Abuse

Child Abuse Prevention, The Lodge, Cherry Orchard
Hospital, Dublin 10, tel. (010) 3531 6232358/6233893
Provides training for the prevention of child abuse.

ChildLine, Freepost 1111 (no stamp needed), London
EC4 4BB, Freefone 0800 1111.
24-hour telephone counselling and advice service for
children in trouble or danger.

Child Protection Societies
Provide help and advice or referral information about
protecting children from child abuse:

**Irish Society for the Prevention of Cruelty to Children
(ISPCC),** 20 Molesworth Street, Dublin 2, tel. (010)
35316794944

**National Society for the Prevention of Cruelty to Children
(NSPCC),** Freefone 0800 800500
24-hour telephone helpline.

**Royal Scottish Society for the Prevention of Cruelty to
Children (RSSPCC),** Melville House, 41 Polworth Terrace,
Edinburgh E11 1NV, tel. (031) 337 8539

Family Contact Line, 30 Church Street, Altrincham,
Cheshire WA14 4DW, tel. (061) 941 4011/4012
Provides a telephone listening service to families. Also has
nursery facilities for parents who wish to attend with their
children.

Kidscape, 152 Buckingham Palace Road, London
SW1W 9TR
Send a large SAE for a free copy of 'Why My Child?', a
28-page booklet for helping parents cope with the sexual
abuse of their child or children. Also available: 'Keep
Them Safe', a 16-page booklet with suggestions for teaching
5- to 11-year-olds ways to stay safe.

AIDS

Your GP or paediatrician should be able to give you advice and can arrange for testing if necessary.

For free leaflets and booklets, contact your local health education unit, listed in the directory under the name of your health authority.

To obtain a copy of 'AIDS: What Everyone Needs to Know', write to: Dept A, PO Box 100, Milton Keynes MK1 1TX.

To obtain a copy of the British Medical Association's 70-page guide entitled 'AIDS and You', send £1.95 to: British Medical Association, Tavistock Square, London WC1H 9JP.

You can also contact:

Health Information Service, Freefone 0800 665544

Health Literature Line, Freefone 0800 555777
Both the above lines are run by the Department of Health.

Health Call, tel. 0898 600 699
Gives recorded general information on AIDS.
Tel. 0898 600 900
Gives recorded specific information on AIDS.

National Aids Helpline, PO Box 1577, London NW1 3DW, helpline 0800 5687123 (24-hour)
All calls are free and confidential and you can call at any time to talk to a trained counsellor.

Terrence Higgins Trust, 52–54 Grays Inn Road, London WC1X 8JU, tel. (071) 831 0330 (10 a.m.–5 p.m. Monday–Friday); helpline (071) 242 1010 (3 p.m.–10 p.m. Monday – Sunday); legal line (071) 405 2381 (7 p.m.–9 p.m. Wednesday)
Offers help and counselling to people with HIV or AIDS.

Positively Women, 5 Sebastian Street, London EC1V 0HE,
helpline (071) 490 2327 (12 p.m.–2 p.m. Monday–Friday)
Provides a range of free and strictly confidential support
services to women with HIV or AIDS. Activities for
women and children, and a children's social worker.

Alcohol

For help with dealing with alcohol abuse contact:

Alcoholics Anonymous, Stonebow House, Stonebow, York
YO1 2NJ, tel. (0904) 644026
Offers helplines:
England   (071) 352 3001 (10 a.m.–10 p.m. Monday–
            Sunday)
Scotland   (041) 221 9027 (24-hour)
Wales   (0646) 695555 (24-hour)
N. Ireland (0232) 681084 (9 a.m.–5 p.m. Monday–Friday)

Al-Anon/Al-Teen, 61 Dover Street, London SE1 4YF, tel.
(071) 403 0888
For family, friends and children who have a relative
affected by drinking problems.

Alcohol Counselling Service (ACS), 34 Electric Lane,
London SW9 8JJ, tel. (071) 737 3579/3570

Drinkline, 13–14 West Smithfield, London EC1A 9DH,
tel. (071) 332 0150; helpline (071) 332 0202
Provides information and advice to callers worried
about their own drinking, offers support to the family
and friends of people who are drinking, and advises
callers on where to go for help.

Anorexia, bulimia and other eating disorders

The following organisations will give advice and/or therapy for people suffering from eating disorders:

Birmingham Women's Therapy Centre, 43 Ladywood, Middleway, Birmingham B16 8HA, tel. (021) 455 8677

Eating Disorders Association (EDA), Sackville Place, 44/48 Magdalen Street, Norwich NR3 1JU, tel. (0603) 621414

The National Centre for Eating Disorders, 11 Esher Place Avenue, Esher, Surrey KT10 8PU, tel. (0372) 469493

The Promis Recovery Centre, Old Court House, Pinners Hill, Nonington, Dover, Kent CT15 4LL, tel. (0304) 841700

Women's Counselling and Therapy Service, Oxford Chambers, Oxford Place, Leeds LS1 3AX, tel. (0532) 455725

Bereavement

The Compassionate Friends, 53 North Street, Bristol BS3 1EN, tel. (0272) 665202; helpline (0272) 539639 (9.30 a.m.–5 p.m. Monday–Friday)
A nationwide (and international) self-help organisation of parents whose children (of any age, including adult) have died through accident, illness, murder or suicide. A postal library and leaflets are also available.

Cruise, 126 Sheen Road, Richmond, Surrey TW9 1UR, helpline (081) 332 7227 (9.30 a.m.–5 p.m. Monday–Friday) Offers counselling for all bereavements.

Bullying

ChildLine, Freefone 0800 1111
24-hour helpline for children to discuss problems, including bullying.

Kidscape, 152 Buckingham Palace Road, London SW1W 9TR, tel. (071) 730 3300
Send a large SAE for a free 20-page booklet entitled 'Stop Bullying!' and other information about schools programmes. Telephone counselling for families available on Mondays and Wednesdays from 9.30 a.m. to 5 p.m.

Contraception

For advice on contraception, pregnancy, or abortion contact:

The British Pregnancy Advisory Service, 7 Belgrave Road, London SW1V 1QB, tel. (071) 222 0985

Brook Advisory Centre (for young people), Head Office, 153A East Street, London SE17 2SD, tel. (071) 708 1234

Family Planning Association, 27 Mortimer Street, London W1N 7RJ, tel. (071) 636 7866

Counselling

These organisations offer counselling on family and other problems.

British Association of Counselling (BAC), 1 Regent Place, Rugby, Warwickshire CV21 2VT
Send A5-size SAE for list of local counsellors. Some are free. Fact sheet available.

Rape Crisis Centre, tel. (071) 837 1600
See directory for local numbers.

Samaritans
See your telephone directory for local numbers.
Samaritans are trained volunteers who talk with people
about problems of depression and suicide.

Women's Therapy Centre, 6 Manor Gardens, London
N7 6LA, helpline (071) 263 6200 (10 a.m.–4 p.m.
Monday–Friday; 2 p.m.–4.30 p.m.–Tuesday, Wednesday
and Thursday)
Send large SAE for list of groups and activities.

Youth Access (formerly NAYPCAS), Magazine Business
Centre, 11 Newarke Street, Leicester LE1 5SS, tel. (0533)
558763
Provides names and addresses of local free counselling
services to young people. Telephone, or write enclosing an
SAE.

Drugs

Doctors, social services, police and Citizens' Advice
Bureaus should be able to advise about drug centres. Dial
100 and ask for Freefone 'Drug Problems'.

Leaflets about drugs are available from: DHSS Leaflets
Unit, Dept DM, PO Box 21, Stanmore, Middlesex
HA7 1AY

* 'What Every Parent Should Know About Drugs'
  (DM1)
* 'Drugs: What Parents Can Do' (DM2)
* 'Drugs Misuse: A Basic Briefing (DM3)
* 'Drugs: What You Can Do as a Parent' (DM4)

The Department of Education and Science and the Welsh
Office also produce leaflets and booklets about drugs,
available in English and Welsh from: The Welsh Office,
Information Division, Cathays Park, Cardiff CF1 3NQ.

To obtain a leaflet on solvent abuse, contact: Solvent
Abuse, Dept M50, 13–39 Standard Road, London
NW10.

- 'What to Do About Glue-sniffing'

You can also contact:

Adfam National, Chapel House, 18 Hatton Place, London
EC1N 8ND, helpline (071) 405 3923 (10 a.m.–5 p.m.
Monday–Friday)
National helpline for the families and friends of drug
users, offering confidential support and information.

Families Anonymous, Unit 37, Doddington & Rollo
Community Association, Charlotte Despart Avenue,
London SW11 5JE, tel. (071) 498 4680
Provides self-help groups for those affected by drug
abuse or its related problems in a relative or friend. It is
completely independent, non-professional and anonymous.

Release, 388 Old Street, London EC1V 9LT, helplines
(071) 729 9904 (10 a.m.–6 p.m. Monday–Friday); (071)
603 8654 (24-hour)
The national drugs and legal advice service. Provides a
24-hour helpline for drug users and their families and
friends.

Society for the Prevention of Solvent Abuse (RESOLV), St
Mary's Chambers, 19 Station Road, Stone, Staffordshire
ST15 8JP, tel. (0785) 817885/46097
Produces teaching programmes to help encourage young
people to resist experimentation. Videos and books
available. For a full list of resources, send a large
SAE.

Standing Conference on Drug Abuse (SCODA), Kingsbury
House, 1–4 Hatton Place, Hatton Garden, London
EC1N 8ND, tel. (071) 430 2341

Will supply a list of local services available throughout the country.

Teachers Advisory Counsel on Alcohol and Drug Education (TACADE), 2 Mount Street, Manchester M2 SN9
Provides education and training materials for the formal education system. Write for full list of materials.

Families

Exploring Parenthood (EP), Latimer Education Centre, 194 Freston Road, London W10 6TT, tel. (081) 960 1678
Provides professional support and advice to all parents who experience problems from time to time. Easy access to professional advice and support.

Family Rights Group (England and Wales), The Print House, 18 Ashwin Street, London E8 3DL, Advice/helpline (071) 249 0008 (1.30 p.m.–3.30 p.m. Monday–Friday)
Promotes partnership between families and child-care agencies in England and Wales. Offers confidential advice on the telephone or by letter.

Parents Anonymous, 6 Manor Gardens, London N7 6LA, tel. (071) 263 8918
Answerphone gives telephone numbers of volunteers who are on duty. They aim to give a 24-hour service.
Offers a listening service plus help and support to parents who are experiencing problems with any issues regarding children and young people.

Parent-Line, Westbury House, 57 Hart Road, Thundersley, Essex SS7 3PP, helpline (0268) 757077 (9 a.m.–6 p.m. Monday–Friday; 10 a.m.–2 p.m. Saturday)
After-hours number supplied on answerphone.
Provides support for parents under stress.

Parent Network, 44–46 Caversham Road, London

NW5 2DS, tel. (071) 485 8535
Programmes to help parents feel supported and
encouraged whilst doing the most important job of raising
children.

Gambling

Gamblers Anonymous and **Gam-Anon,** PO Box 88, London
SW10 0EU, helpline (071) 384 3040 (24-hour)
Gamblers Anonymous is a self-help group of men
and women who have joined together to do something
about their gambling problems. Gam-Anon offers
friendship, practical help, comfort and understanding to
families of compulsive gamblers.

UK Forum on Young People and Gambling, 11 St Bride
Street, London EC4 4AS, contact name Paul Bellringer,
tel. (0243) 538635
Offers advice to parents and young people with gambling
problems. Also offers advice to young people addicted to
video games.

Legal advice

The Children's Legal Centre, 20 Compton Terrace, London
N1 2UN, helpline (071) 359 6251 (2 p.m.–5 p.m. Monday–
Friday)
Gives advice about law and policy affecting children and
young people in England and Wales.

Citizens' Advice Bureaus
Telephone numbers are listed in local directories.
Will give details of services available and advice on how
to get help.

Self-defence

Contact your local council or the library for information
about self-defence classes in your area.

The Suzy Lamplugh Trust, 14 East Sheen Avenue, London
SW14 8AS, tel. (081) 392 1839
Produces material such as videos and leaflets about
keeping safe and self-defence, particularly aimed at
those who work with the public and who may find
themselves in a dangerous situation.

Suicide

ChildLine, Freefone 0800 1111
24-hour helpline for children to discuss any problem.

Kidscape, 152 Buckingham Palace Road, London
SW1W 9TR
Kidscape has a free leaflet entitled 'Suicide and Young
People'. For a copy, send a large SAE.

Samaritans
See your telephone directory for local numbers.
   The Samaritans run 24-hour helplines to listen to any
problems, including feeling suicidal.

Telephone services

To register complaints about any telephone service lines
run by BT, Freefone 0800 500 212 (helpline).

To arrange to block telephone service line numbers
so that they cannot be dialled from your telephone,
Freefone 0800 800 810 (helpline).

A leaflet entitled 'Nuisance Callers', giving guidance on
how to deal with abusive or nuisance telephone calls
and what BT can do to help, is available free from BT
Customer Service.

Victim support

Victim Support Scheme, National Office, Cranmer House,
39 Brixton Road, London SW9 6DZ, tel. (071) 735 9166
A nationwide network of support groups offering practical
help and advice to victims of violence and crime. You can
find out the number of your local branch by contacting
the office listed above or by looking in your local
directory.

APPENDIX I

'WHAT IF?' QUESTIONS

The following 'What if?' questions are ways to continue conversations with your children and teenagers about safety issues. Obviously, you will need to decide which questions to raise, depending on the age and maturity level of your children. Discussing and thinking about what to do is more valuable than being told the 'right' answers. In some situations, there are no right answers. Take care not to overdo them; my eldest son declared 'No more "What ifs?", Mum, please!' Nonetheless, we must continue to discuss these subjects until keeping safe becomes second nature.

> One mother rang to say that her eleven-year-old son was on his way home from school when he was confronted by a stranger who tried to pull him into a car. He yelled and ran, went to the police station and gave a description of the car and the man. When he was questioned, the boy said that he knew what to do because he'd been 'Kidscaped'. His mother said that she was delighted, but also wanted us to know that her son had professed extreme boredom with the whole topic of safety whenever she brought it up. After the incident, however, he wanted us to know that he 'really wasn't bored and that the "What if?" questions had helped'.

Having children decide on their own questions in groups has been used very successfully in many classrooms. Some families make 'What if?' into a game. Use this section to continue the process of getting children and young people to think for themselves.

'What if?' questions to ask your children

WHAT IF . . .

*   You are being bullied by someone at school who has made you promise not to tell?

*   You see a friend steal something from a shop?

*   A friend of yours tells you a secret that makes you feel unsafe and makes you promise not to tell?

*   Your mum asks you to keep your brother's birthday present a secret?

*   You are on your way home and you are being followed? You are in a street with only houses and no shops. You do not know anyone who lives around there

*   You are staying with a babysitter and the doorbell rings? The sitter tells you to answer it

*   You notice a fire in the kitchen while Dad has just popped out to the papershop?

*   You see someone you don't know steal something from a shop?

*   You are grabbed by someone and pulled into a car? The person has you in the front seat of the car and tells you not to do anything

*   You are in the toilet at a restaurant and a person shows you their private parts and offers you a sweet 'not to tell'?

*   A grown-up tells you to run across the road, even though there are cars coming?

- Your dog runs into the road and there is a car coming?

- You come home from school to find the front door open and things scattered all over the house?

- You get separated from your parents in a shop? In the park?

- You see a flasher?

- You get an upsetting phone call in which someone says dirty words?

- You see a syringe on the ground?

- A grown-up or teenager asks you to keep a touch a secret?

- You are scared of the dark?

- You hate the babysitter but are frightened to tell your parents?

- A man and woman drive up in a lovely car and ask you for directions?

- Your little sister/brother is being bullied by someone you know?

- You and your brother are planning a surprise for your mum's birthday and promise each other not to tell. Should you tell your mum?

- You are home alone and a delivery man comes to the door with some groceries and asks to be let in? If a person with a large bunch of flowers comes? The milkman? The postman? Your cousin? Your sister?

- A stranger says your mum is ill and offers to take you home?

- Your mum says you have to kiss someone goodbye, but you don't want to because you're shy or you just don't feel like it?

- You see a fire in your neighbour's house?

- You are alone and the telephone rings? The man wants to talk to your father?

- A person comes to the door and says there is an emergency? The person asks to use the telephone and you are at home alone?

- Someone you know always tickles you and you hate it?

- You are in a wheelchair and people keep patting you on the head, even though you don't like it?

- You have to stay with a relative who makes you feel really uncomfortable? You have to try to explain to your mum?

- You have your bike stolen by a gang of bullies who warn you not to tell 'or else'?

- You are taking a short cut through the park, which your parents have told you not to do? A man follows/grabs you, says/does rude things and makes you promise not to tell. You know your parents will be angry because you shouldn't have gone into the park alone

- Friends of yours offer you some powder to swallow, saying it will make you feel wonderful?

- A policeman comes to your door and asks to come in while you are on your own? (Police officers carry warrant cards and are obliged to produce them when asked. Although this verifies their identity, children should not let *anyone* in if they are alone.)

'What if?' questions to ask your teens

WHAT IF . . .
- Someone offers you drugs?

- You get on a bus and the person next to you starts whispering obscenities to you?

- A bully makes you pay them money every day?

- You are abducted and are riding along in a car with your abductor?

- Someone you met at a disco offers to take you home?

- A boy/girl you know wants to sleep with you? If you know they have a reputation for sleeping around?

- You are being followed on a street late at night? There are houses, but no one seems to be up

- You are being followed as you jog in the park?

- You are grabbed from behind by someone with a weapon?

- You find out a friend has AIDS and he/she is planning to sleep with another friend of yours who does not know?

- You receive an obscene telephone call when you are home alone? The caller says he can see you and threatens you?

- You are babysitting and the doorbell rings? You look through the peephole and see a delivery man with flowers?

- You are invited to a party when your friend's parents are out of town? You suspect the parents would be furious if they knew

- A friend of yours is being abused and tells you, but asks you not to tell anyone else?

- You are alone working in a shop when a robber comes in and demands the money in the till?

- You are on your paper round and a car starts following you slowly?

- You are babysitting and the person driving you home is drunk? It is very late and your parents are asleep at home?

- You see a stranger steal something from a shop?

- You see your best friend steal something from a shop?

- You are in a public toilet and the man next to you tries to molest you?

- You are babysitting and a small fire breaks out in the kitchen? The children are asleep upstairs

- You get drunk at a party, but your parents don't know you are even at a party? You need to go home

- You are offered a chance to see a pornographic video with some friends?

- You are in a video arcade when a man comes up to you and offers to pay for your games because he likes young people and has grandchildren your age?

- A friend of your offers you some cocaine and urges you to try it just once? He or she says you're a coward if you don't and it is only an experiment

- You are walking home from the bus when a man and woman in a car pull up to ask you for directions?

- A friend or relative of yours tries to touch you in a way you don't like?

- You find out your little brother or sister is sniffing glue and he/she begs you not to tell?

- You are in a lift and the door is just closing when a person gets in who makes you feel very uncomfortable?

- A relative or friend of yours has a drinking problem?

- You feel suicidal?

- You think there is no one to talk to who would understand you?

- A friend confides that he/she is a drug addict? You're the only one who knows and you've promised to keep it a secret

- Your little sister tells you that she is being bullied at school and doesn't want to go any more?
- Friends tell you they are going out to get drunk and plan to drive home? You are invited, but sworn to secrecy
- You come home alone to find the door to your flat open and hear the sound of things being broken?
- Someone flashes at you?
- While you are in a place your parents have forbidden, you are assaulted, robbed, etc? You think your parents will be furious with you and never let you out again

APPENDIX II

QUESTIONNAIRE FOR YOUNG TEENAGERS

This questionnaire is designed to be used as a tool for communicating with young people about keeping safe from assault. It is not meant to be a test that is marked, but a way of opening up the subject without being alarmist. You may not always agree with the answers; some could be true or false depending on the circumstances. The answers are given as a guide.

The questionnaire does not mention sex abuse or rape, but does use the word assault. It can be used with younger or less mature teens. The questionnaire in Appendix III is for older teens.

Questions

1. You have the right to be safe.   **T F**

2. You should always keep secrets if you promise not to tell.   **T F**

3. A bribe is given to make you do something you do not want to do.   **T F**

4. People are either good or bad.   **T F**

5. Only bad people who look strange hurt children.   **T F**

6. Adults do not always believe children.   **T F**

7. Children should always obey adults.   **T F**

8. You sometimes have the right to break rules.   **T F**

9. It is a good idea to answer the telephone by repeating your name or your telephone number.   **T F**

10. You should never lie.   **T F**

11. You should never fight back if someone attacks you.   **T F**

12. You have the right to tell anyone, even someone you know and trust, not to touch you in any way that makes you feel uncomfortable.   **T F**

13. Jealousy is a sign of true love.   **T F**

14. You should never hurt anyone's feelings.   **T F**

15. Looking foolish in front of others is really embarrassing.   **T F**

16. Boys are usually encouraged to be sensitive and gentle with girls.   **T F**

17. When a child is assaulted, the offender is usually a stranger.   **T F**

18. Girls are assaulted much more often than boys.   **T F**

19. The vast majority of attackers are men.   **T F**

20. The best way to escape a potential assault is to vomit.   **T F**

21. A 'real man' shows the girl that he is the boss.   **T F**

22. Generally the more attractive a girl is the greater her chance of being assaulted.   **T F**

23. It is sometimes the victim's fault that he/she was assaulted.   **T F**

24. People are much safer from assault at home.   **T F**

25. If you or someone you know is assaulted, you should tell a trusted adult immediately.   **T F**

Answers

1. You have the right to be safe. **True**

2. You should always keep secrets if you promise not to tell. **False**
   Some secrets should not be kept. If anyone asks you to keep touching a secret or if you feel confused, uncomfortable or frightened by a secret, find a trusted adult to tell.

3. A bribe is given to make you do something you do not want to do. **True**

4. People are either good or bad. **False**

5. Only bad people who look strange hurt children. **False**

6. Adults do not always believe children. **True**
   If the first person you tell a problem to does not believe you, keep telling until someone does.

7. Children should always obey adults. **False**
   In order to keep safe, it may be necessary to disobey an adult.

8. You sometimes have the right to break rules. **True**
   To keep safe, you have the right to break any rules.

9. It is a good idea to answer the telephone by repeating your name or your telephone number. **False**

10. You should never lie. **False**
    You might have to lie to keep safe. For example, you could say that your mum was waiting for you across the road if someone was bothering you.

11. You should never fight back if someone attacks you. **False**
    If you feel in danger, you should do whatever you can to keep safe, such as kick, yell, bite, etc.

12. You have the right to tell anyone, even some-
    one you know and trust, not to touch you in
    any way which makes you feel uncomfortable.   **True**
    You have the right to say who touches your body.

13. Jealousy is a sign of true love.   **False**
    Love depends upon mutual trust. Jealousy is
    based upon lack of trust.

14. You should never hurt anyone's feelings.   **False**
    In order to keep yourself safe, you may have to
    say no to someone you know and like, which
    might hurt his or her feelings.

15. Looking foolish in front of others is really
    embarrassing.   **True**
    But do not be afraid to look foolish if you feel
    inside that something is wrong. If you think you
    should leave a party, for example, because you
    do not like what is happening, do leave even if
    you are embarrassed. It might keep you safe.

16. Boys are usually encouraged to be sensitive and
    gentle with girls.   **False**
    Girls should make it clear to boys that they like
    boys who are not afraid to be kind. Boys often
    think that girls only like the 'macho' type.

17. When a child is assaulted, the offender is usually
    a stranger.   **False**
    More than 75 per cent of people who assault
    children are known to the children.

18. Girls are assaulted much more often than boys.   **False**
    Boys are almost as much at risk as girls, although
    they report assaults less often.

19. The vast majority of assaults are committed by
    men.   **True**
    More than 90 per cent of reported assaults are
    committed by men. However, most men would
    never attack anyone.

20. The best way to escape a potential assault is to vomit. **False**
While it may work, conversations with offenders indicate that these kinds of tactics make them angry rather than disgusted. Many people feel that an immediate spirited physical self-defence, including loud yelling, kicking, hitting, etc., is best because the element of surprise helps the victim to get away. Some people have successfully talked their way out of dangerous situations. Each person must decide what is best according to the circumstances.

21. A 'real man' shows the girl that he is the boss. **False**
Why should one partner be boss?

22. Generally the more attractive a girl is the greater her chance of being assaulted. **False**
Studies have shown that being physically attractive has nothing to do with assault.

23. It is sometimes the victim's fault that he/she was assaulted. **False**
It is always the offender's fault. No one deserves to be assaulted.

24. People are much safer from assault at home. **False**
In a recent London survey, 51 per cent of assaults happened either in the victim's or the assailant's home.

25. If you or someone you know is assaulted, you should tell a trusted adult immediately. **True**
Think about people who would believe you and who would help you make a decision about what to do. An assault is too big a burden to carry in secret and getting help early will often lessen the trauma.

APPENDIX III

QUESTIONNAIRE FOR OLDER TEENAGERS

One way to begin talking with young people about keeping safe from sexual abuse and assault is to give them this questionnaire or for them to take it with them. It is not meant to be a quiz to be marked, but a basis for communication. Although answers are given, in some cases you may disagree with the answer. The desired outcome should be that teenagers think about and plan what to do should they be placed in a dangerous situation. This isn't a contest to get the 'right' answer.

This questionnaire does mention the terms sex abuse and rape and should be used with more mature teenagers.

Questions

1. You have the right to tell anyone, even someone you know and trust, not to touch you in any way that makes you feel uncomfortable.   **T F**

2. When a girl says 'no' to a boy, she frequently means 'yes'.   **T F**

3. A boy has a right to expect more than a kiss after he has spent money on a date.   **T F**

4. Jealousy is a sign of true love.   **T F**

5. Birth control is the female's responsibility.   **T F**

6. Boys are not encouraged to be sensitive and gentle with girls. **T F**

7. Sexual frustration can be physically harmful. **T F**

8. People who fantasise about being seduced or raped have emotional problems. **T F**

9. Most date rapes occur because a girl teases a boy to the point that he cannot control himself. **T F**

10. Alcohol and/or drugs can lower inhibitions about engaging in sexual activity. **T F**

11. When a child is molested, the molester is usually a stranger. **T F**

12. Girls are molested much more often than boys. **T F**

13. The vast majority of sexual abusers are men. **T F**

14. The best way to escape a potential rapist is to vomit. **T F**

15. A 'real man' shows the girl that he is the boss. **T F**

16. Generally the more attractive a girl is the higher her chance of being sexually assaulted. **T F**

17. When a girl is sexually assaulted, she has usually done something to provoke it. **T F**

18. It is against the law for a boy to engage in sexual intercourse with a girl under sixteen, even with her consent. **T F**

19. Sexual gratification is the major reason for rape. **T F**

20. Males who are sexually assaulted suffer the same kind of emotional trauma as female victims. **T F**

21. People are much safer from sexual assault at home. **T F**

22. Less than half of all rapes are reported to the police. **T F**

23. An assailant rarely finds it necessary to use a weapon to commit rape. **T F**

24. People who sexually assault others are psychologically disturbed. **T F**

25. Rapists are secret, solitary offenders who usually attack their victims when the rapist is alone. **T F**

26. Teenage and adult victims of sexual assault seldom know the identity of the offender. **T F**

27. Sexual assault is usually an unplanned, spontaneous act. **T F**

28. There are many false reports of rape by women seeking revenge on their boyfriends. **T F**

29. If a female victim feels uncomfortable talking with a male police officer, she has the right to request that a female officer be called. **T F**

30. Since the rape victim is often unprotected by contraceptives, she will probably become pregnant. **T F**

31. The victim is allowed to have a friend stay with her during the medical examination or questioning. **T F**

32. During an investigation of rape, the victim can refuse to answer questions irrelevant to the rape. **T F**

33. If a woman is raped, her name will be published by the media reporting her case. **T F**

34. As a rule, the rape victim can be asked questions in court about her sexual conduct. **T F**

35. If you or someone you know has been sexually assaulted, you should tell a trusted adult immediately. **T F**

Answers

1. You have the right to tell anyone, even someone you know and trust, not to touch you in
   any way that makes you feel uncomfortable.   **True**
   **Since a high percentage of the assaults on teen-
   agers are by an adult known to them, it is important to learn to say no not only to strangers, but
   to friends, family members or acquaintances.**

2. When a girl says 'no' to a boy, she frequently
   means 'yes'.   **False**
   **This attitude is left over from old films and
   books. Boys and girls should discuss together
   their ideas about mixed messages to that each
   understands the expectations and the misconcep-
   tions of the other.**

3. A boy has a right to expect more than a kiss
   after he has spent money on a date.   **False**
   If this is his attitude, 'go Dutch'.

4. Jealousy is a sign of true love.   **False**
   **Love depends upon mutual trust. Jealousy is
   based upon lack of trust.**

5. Birth control is the female's responsibility.   **False**
   It should be a shared responsibility.

6. Boys are not encouraged to be sensitive and
   gentle with girls.   **True**
   **Most boys are raised to believe that being tough
   and macho is what girls expect of them. This
   should be discussed so that girls and boys can
   decide what they value in a relationship.**

7. Sexual frustration can be physically harmful.   **False**
   Boys have used this line for years!

8. People who fantasise about being seduced or
   raped have emotional problems.   **False**

Some people have 'seduction' fantasies. In the fantasy, they are in control; they choose the 'assailant', place, circumstances, etc. The reality of rape is different – violent and sadistic.

9. Most date rapes occur because a girl teases the boy to the point that he cannot control himself.   **False**
   This attitude blames the victim. Rape occurs because the assailant has problems with anger, aggression, hostility and power.

10. Alcohol and/or drugs can lower inhibitions about engaging in sexual activity.   **True**
    Studies have shown this to be true for both sexes.

11. When a child is molested, the molester is usually a stranger.   **False**
    The child knows the attacker in at least 75 per cent of reported cases of child molestation.

12. Girls are molested much more often than boys.   **False**
    Statistics vary, but boys are almost as much at risk as girls. The victimisation of boys is reported less often, partly because of the fear of being branded as a homosexual after an attack.

13. The vast majority of sexual abusers are men.   **True**
    Ninety per cent of reported attacks are committed by men.

14. The best way to escape a potential rapist is to vomit.   **False**
    While it may work, conversations with convicted rapists indicate that these kinds of tactics make them angry rather than disgusted. Many people feel that an immediate spirited physical defence, including loud yelling, kicking, hitting, etc., is best because the element of surprise would

help the victim to get away. Some people have successfully talked their way out of rape, but each must decide for herself according to the circumstances.

15. A 'real man' shows the girls that he is the boss.   **False**
Why should one partner be the boss? This implies that the girl is incapable of directing her own life. It places her in the same category as a docile pet.

16. Generally the more attractive a girl is the higher her chance of being sexually assaulted.   **False**
Studies of assault victims have shown that being physically attractive has nothing to do with sexual assault.

17. When a girl is sexually assaulted, she has usually done something to provoke it.   **False**
In the United States, the National Commission on the Causes and Prevention of Violence did a study on crimes of violence and paid particular attention to the role of the victim in cases of murder, assault, robbery and rape. The commission wanted to determine whether victims of these crimes in any way provoked them or rashly touched off the action against them. It was discovered that victims of rape were less responsible for provocative behaviour or unwitting collusion than were victims of murder, assault or robbery. The cases on file of rapes of individuals of all ages, from three-month-old babies to ninety-seven-year-old women, show how ridiculous this myth really is.

18. It is against the law for a boy to engage in sexual intercourse with a girl under sixteen, even with her consent.   **True**
The legal age of consent is sixteen.

19. Sexual gratification is the major reason for rape. **False**
    Rape is about violence, not sex. If you hit someone over the head with your rolling pin, it is not called cooking.

20. Males who are sexually assaulted suffer the same kind of emotional trauma as female victims. **True**
    Sexual assault on males is reported even less often than assault on females and there is no support system, such as Rape Crisis Centres, for male victims.

21. People are much safer from sexual assault at home. **False**
    In a recent London survey, 51 per cent of sexual assaults happened in either the victim's or the assailant's home.

22. Less than half of all rapes are reported to the police. **True**
    Only one in twelve are reported, according to a London survey.

23. An assailant rarely finds it necessary to use a weapon to commit rape. **True**
    Only a small proportion of sexual assaults involve weapons. Most assailants use superior size and fear to subdue victims.

24. People who sexually assault others are psychologically disturbed. **False**
    Most test as 'normal' on psychological tests.

25. Rapists are secret, solitary offenders who usually attack their victims when the rapist is alone. **True**
    In only one in a hundred cases in a London survey was there more than one assailant.

26. Teenage and adult victims seldom know the identity of the rapist.   **False**
   In a London survey, more than 60 per cent of attackers were known to the victim.

27. Sexual assault is usually an unplanned, spontaneous act.   **False**
   Most sexual assaults are planned.

28. There are many false reports of rape by women seeking revenge on their boyfriends.   **False**
   In a study in New York of all the reported rapes in one year, only 2 per cent turned out to be false.

29. If a female victim feels uncomfortable talking with a male police officer, she has the right to request that a female officer be called.   **True**
   While a victim has the right to request this, the police have no obligation to provide a female officer. The police do try to comply with this request if at all possible.

30. Since the rape victim is often unprotected by contraceptives, she will probably become pregnant.   **False**
   Only a small percentage of rape victims become pregnant.

31. The victim is allowed to have a friend stay with her during the medical examination or questioning.   **True**
   This can be a family member or close friend.

32. During an investigation of a rape, the victim can refuse to answer questions irrelevant to the rape.   **True**
   Questions about a victim's personal life, not relevant to the rape, need not be answered.

33. If a woman is raped, her name will be published by the media reporting her case.   **False**

Rape victims are entitled to anonymity before, during and after the trial.

34. As a rule, the rape victim can be asked questions in court about her sexual conduct.   **False**
    In court a rape victim may not be asked questions about her previous sexual conduct unless the judge is satisfied that these questions are relevant to the defence.

35. If you or someone you know has been sexually assaulted, you should tell a trusted adult immediately.   **True**
    Think about the people who would believe you and who would help you in making a decision about what to do. Sexual assault is too big a burden to carry in secret and getting supportive help early will often lessen the trauma. If you feel completely alone, telephone your local Rape Crisis Centre or the Samaritans (numbers in the telephone directory) or ChildLine (0800 1111).

APPENDIX IV

SOURCES OF INFORMATION

Books for children

TITLE: **The Body Book** (ages 4 to 11)
AUTHOR: Claire Rayner
PUBLISHER: Piccolo Books
Brilliantly simple explanation about how the body works.
Clear, friendly language and illustrations make this a delight
to use with children.

TITLE: **Boy** (ages 8 to adult)
AUTHOR: Roald Dahl
PUBLISHER: Penguin
Into his description of a charmed childhood spent in Wales
and Norway, the author weaves the story of the cruel and
barbaric treatment he received at an English public school.

TITLE: **Bully** (ages 3 to 7)
AUTHOR: David Hughes
PUBLISHER: Walker Books
Dogs, pigs, cats, penguins and children all deal with bullying
in this big, wonderfully illustrated colour picture book.

TITLE: **The Bullies Meet the Willow Street Kids** (ages
                    7 to 11)
AUTHOR: Michele Elliott
PUBLISHER: Pan

In this sequel to *The Willow Street Kids*, it is not only Marilyn who finds herself the victim of bullying at the new school: Gill, Charlie and the rest also encounter Liz and her gang, both in and out of school.

TITLE: **Feeling Happy, Feeling Safe** (ages 3 to 7)
AUTHOR: Michele Elliott
PUBLISHER: Hodder/Headline
A brightly illustrated colour picture book with short stories about getting lost, strangers, bullies, secrets and other safety themes for young children. Includes notes for parents.

TITLE: **No More Bullying!** (ages 4 to 6)
AUTHOR: Rosemary Stones
PUBLISHER: Dinosaur
Colour picture book about a girl who learns to cope with bullying.

TITLE: **The Willow Street Kids** (ages 7 to 11)
AUTHOR: Michele Elliott
PUBLISHER: Pan
Based on true stories of children's experiences and written in an entertaining way, this book will help children figure out what to do in a variety of situations – bullying, getting lost, stranger danger and unwelcome advances from known adults. Chosen for the 'Good Book Guide'.

Books for teens

TITLE: **Bullies**
AUTHOR: Ed Wise
PUBLISHER: Kingsway
Alex was the world's greatest expert on bullies. One night, after dealing with the bullies, Alex had a dream . . . In the end, the bullies didn't stand a chance.

TITLE: **Bully**
AUTHOR: Yvonne Coppard
PUBLISHER: Bodley Head

Kerry knew it would happen again – the bullies would be waiting at the gate. Alone and friendless, she is a prime target for the bullies. But Kerry eventually triumphs.

TITLE: **Don't Pick on Me: How to Handle Bullying**
AUTHOR: Rosemary Stones
PUBLISHER: Piccadilly Press
This book discusses why people bully and what you can do to change things. It incorporates several of the Kidscape suggestions to stop bullying.

TITLE: **Out in the Open: A Guide for Young People Who Have Been Sexually Abused**
AUTHOR: Ouaine Bain and Maureen Sanders
PUBLISHER: Virago
A useful book for young people to help them come to terms with having been abused.

TITLE: **Too Close Encounters and What to Do About Them**
AUTHOR: Rosemary Stones
PUBLISHER: Methuen
Based on common sense, with practical strategies for dealing with everything from flashers to rape, this guide is full of valuable ideas for young people.

Books for adults

TITLE: **Alcohol, Smoking, Tranquillisers**
AUTHOR: Hasnain Walji and Dr Andrea Kingston
PUBLISHER: Hodder/Headline
Provides a simple and practical introduction to addictions and what to do about treating this dependency.

TITLE: **Anorexia Nervosa: A Guide for Sufferers and Their Families**
AUTHOR: R. L. Palmer
PUBLISHER: Penguin

Discusses the causes, symptoms and treatment of anorexia in light of current medical opinion. Practical suggestions for dealing with the problem.

TITLE:　　　**Bullying: A Practical Guide to Coping for Schools**
AUTHOR:　　Michele Elliott (ed.)
PUBLISHER: Longman
Provides practical ideas for teachers and other school personnel to use in dealing with bullying. It explores ways to help bullies and victims, strategies for schools, and gives suggestions for playgrounds and how to set up 'bully courts'.

TITLE:　　　**Bullying at School: What We Know and What We Can Do**
AUTHOR:　　Dan Olweus
PUBLISHER: Blackwell
This book from the recognised international expert in the field of bullying gives effective ways of counteracting and preventing bullying. The facts about bullying, its causes and consequences are clearly presented.

TITLE:　　　**Caring for the Suicidal**
AUTHOR:　　John Eldrid
PUBLISHER: Constable
From the director of the Central London branch of the Samaritans, this book is based on years of experience and is full of practical, down-to-earth advice.

TITLE:　　　**Child Abuse: The Developing Child**
AUTHOR:　　Ruth S. Kempe and C. Henry Kempe
PUBLISHER: Fontana
Clearly written, comprehensive guide to understanding child abuse.

TITLE:　　　**The Common Secret: Sexual Abuse of Children**
AUTHOR:　　Ruth S. Kempe and C. Henry Kempe
PUBLISHER: Freeman
From the respected pioneers in the field of child abuse, this book examines child sexual abuse in all its forms, from paedophilia to child pornography to incest.

TITLE: **Cry Hard and Swim**
AUTHOR: Jacqueline Spring
PUBLISHER: Virago
In letters to her mother, poems and narrative, the painful story of father–daughter incest emerges. Through therapy and hard work, Jacqueline heals herself and helps others.

TITLE: **Drug Warning**
AUTHOR: David Stockley
PUBLISHER: Optima
An illustrated guide for parents and teachers, giving information on treatment and where to get help.

TITLE: **Female Sexual Abuse of Children: The Ultimate Taboo**
AUTHOR: Michele Elliott (ed.)
PUBLISHER: Longman
In this pioneering study, the testimony of survivors, and of the professionals who have worked with them and with the abusers, bears witness to the sexual abuse of children by women.

TITLE: **Fighting, Teasing and Bullying**
AUTHOR: Dr John Pearce
PUBLISHER: Thorsons
If your child is a victim of bullying or a bully, this book will help you to recognise the problems. Useful strategies to help children learn self-confidence.

TITLE: **For Your Own Good: The Roots of Violence in Child Rearing**
AUTHOR: Alice Miller
PUBLISHER: Virago
Explores attitudes that emphasise discipline and obedience and the links to such authoritarians as Hitler, who was abused as a child.

TITLE: **Helping Children Cope with Stress**
AUTHOR: Ursula Markham
PUBLISHER: Sheldon Press

Helps you to recognise the symptoms of stress and offers advice for particular problems and for generally equipping children to deal with stressful situations.

TITLE: **How to Stand Up for Yourself**
AUTHOR: Dr Paul Hauck
PUBLISHER: Sheldon Press
How to feel good about yourself and get your own way without taking advantage of other people is the basis of this very useful little book.

TITLE: **Substance Dependency: A Professional Guide**
AUTHOR: Andrew Shephard
PUBLISHER: Venture Press
A guide to new approaches to dealing with dependency on drugs, solvents and alcohol. The author explores ways to overcome dependency and the reasons why people become addicted.

TITLE: **Victims No Longer**
AUTHOR: Mike Lew
PUBLISHER: Cedar Books/Heinemann
An essential book for men and boys who are survivors of sexual abuse. It breaks down one of the final barriers and helps men to come to terms with their feelings.

Training package for front-line carers

TITLE: **Protecting Children: Training Pack for Front-Line Carers**
AUTHOR: Michele Elliott
PUBLISHER: HMSO
Sponsored by the Department of Health, this package consists of a manual and video to help front-line carers such as foster parents, teachers, health visitors and others to understand the problem of child abuse and to have practical ways to help children who have been abused. Available from Kidscape.

Kidscape child-protection school programmes

TITLE: **Kidscape Child Protection Programme** (ages 5–11)
AUTHOR: Michele Elliott
PUBLISHER: Kidscape

Comprehensive personal safety programme that deals with getting lost, bullying, stranger danger, and potential abuse from known adults. Includes an illustrative video for adults, lessons, exercises and follow-up activities for children, posters, leaflets and ideas for adapting and using the materials with children of different abilities and with special educational needs.

TITLE: **Kidscape Under-Fives Manual**
AUTHOR: Michele Elliott
PUBLISHER: Kidscape

Provides lessons for young children and for children for whom English is a second language. It is also appropriate for children with special educational needs.

TITLE: **Teenscape**
AUTHOR: Michele Elliott
PUBLISHER: Health Education Authority

A complete programme for teenagers dealing with issues of personal safety, child abuse, crime, responsibilities, gambling, addiction and bullying.

Talking books for the blind

TITLE: **Preventing Child Sexual Assault**
AUTHOR: Michele Elliott
CATALOGUE NO: T5548/2 cassettes

Practical advice about talking with children. Available from Royal National Institute for the Blind Library, tel. (0345) 023153.